Motivation And Power Sources

MAPS to the Present Moment

Guidebook

Sande Craig

BALBOA.
PRESS

A DIVISION OF HAY HOUSE

Balboa Press books may be ordered through booksellers or by contacting:

Balboa Press
A Division of Hay House
1663 Liberty Drive
Bloomington, IN 47403
www.balboapress.com
1 (877) 407-4847

Because of the dynamic nature of the Internet, any web addresses or links contained in this book may have changed since publication and may no longer be valid. The views expressed in this work are solely those of the author and do not necessarily reflect the views of the publisher, and the publisher hereby disclaims any responsibility for them.

The author of this book does not dispense medical advice or prescribe the use of any technique as a form of treatment for physical, emotional, or medical problems without the advice of a physician, either directly or indirectly. The intent of the author is only to offer information of a general nature to help you in your quest for emotional and spiritual well-being. In the event you use any of the information in this book for yourself, which is your constitutional right, the author and the publisher assume no responsibility for your actions.

Any people depicted in stock imagery provided by Thinkstock are models, and such images are being used for illustrative purposes only.
Certain stock imagery © Thinkstock.

Print information available on the last page.

ISBN: 978-1-5043-2743-5 (sc)
ISBN: 978-1-5043-2744-2 (e)

Library of Congress Control Number: 2015902848

Balboa Press rev. date: 04/10/2015

Willingness is the key that unlocks the door to change.

If you want to change your mind, mood, attitude, thoughts, feelings, perceptions, beliefs, habits, etc., willingness is the first step.

Do you want peace of mind and heart or do you want to hang on to that old anger, sadness, resentment, guilt, fear, and mental suffering in all the forms it takes?

If you are willing to let go of what keeps you unhappy, then here are some MAPS into the present moment, where change can happen.

This little guidebook is full of ways to help you think and feel better in order to live a healthier, happier life.

Discover your MAPS to the present moment and make the changes you want for yourself.

Boundless blessings!

To my three wonderful Sons and their Dad. Thank you.

"Our true home is the present moment.
To live in the present moment is a miracle.
The miracle is not to walk on water.
The miracle is to walk on the green Earth in the present moment,
To appreciate the peace and beauty that are available now.
Peace is all around us—
In the world and in nature—
And within us—
In our bodies and our spirits.
Once we learn to touch this peace, we will be healed and transformed.
It is not a matter of faith;
It is a matter of practice.
We need only to find ways to bring our body and
mind back to the present moment
So we can touch what is refreshing, healing and wondrous."

—Thich Nhat Hanh, *Touching Peace: Practicing the Art of Mindful Living*

♥   ♥   ♥

Contents

Preface

The information in this guidebook has been revealed to me throughout my life. But in 2006, I was guided to begin writing this.

I remember as a child going almost daily to the meadow (which fortunately was right across the street from my house), climbing trees and rocks, gazing at the clouds, talking with God and angels, and feeling comforted by nature's embrace.

Growing up had its difficulties, but somehow I had an awareness that I was not alone. There have been many times in my life when I felt lonely, but deep within me, there has been the knowledge that I am supported by unseen energy and love, and when I forget, something always brings me back to remembering.

As a kid, I occasionally went to a Presbyterian church, and throughout my teens I explored the Catholic religion, Judaism, and later, Taoism, Buddhism, Hinduism, and more. I've always loved going to different churches and temples and feeling God's presence everywhere. Most often, church for me is outside, in Mother Nature's arms.

My godmother and I shared a very special spiritual connection. She experienced many encounters with her angels during her life, and one of the most beautiful was when she heard God say to her, "Child of Mine and dear to Me, thus have I fashioned thee, joyous, gracious, glad, and free." Whenever I think of her, these words speak to me and continue to be a source of motivation and power.

I've exposed myself to many belief systems and have been touched deeply by Rumi and Hafiz. The teachings and writings of Paramahansa

Yogananda led me to a deeper understanding of Jesus' teachings, the Christ Consciousness, meditation, and a deep appreciation of my path.

So many wise ones have lit the way along my life's path and journey. There are too many to mention here, but I am so grateful for their wisdom, which has given me aha moments and validation of truths, insights, and realizations.

Exploring many metaphysical and esoteric teachings throughout my life has enhanced my experience of God's presence in the form of miracles and blessings. Some of the most profound of these are my relationships with angels, guides, helpers, healers, masters, and teachers, in physical and nonphysical form, as they have revealed themselves to me.

After many years of meditation, countless workshops, hundreds of books, life lessons, grace, and higher guidance, I was finally ready to commit to a daily practice of energization exercises and meditation that has carried me, supported me, and sustained me for the past forty-plus years.

I have found that daily rituals and routines help me stay centered and in a state of gratitude and appreciation. Each morning when I walk, I am thankful for the beauty I see and the heartfelt appreciation of life that I feel.

As we experience daily life, we come across and gather pearls of insight, wisdom, and grace. A line in a movie or a book, a spectacular sunset, working in the garden on a warm spring morning, a day off with your child, and lunch with a friend are just a few examples of where inspiration comes. These are the present moments where we can access our MAPS.

All of the MAPS ideas, materials, etc. have been Divinely inspired. I am humbled and grateful to have been given this information and to share it with you.

I thank God and my enlightened Angels, Guides, Helpers, Healers, Masters, and Teachers, who assist me on my journey and shine their Light on my path every day.

I want to thank and acknowledge some Earth angels who are so helpful and important to me:

My three sons, Carl Anthony, Kevin, and Django Craig, for their love and wisdom, and for constantly cheering me on. Their love lifts me up.

Linda Sainz, for her wise input and unending, loving encouragement. From the beginning, she has taken these ideas and used them with her students, colleagues, friends, and herself, with much success. She has been the copilot of this work. Her Angels and Guides are continually working in concert with mine to offer this material to you.

Eileen Kenny, for her huge heart, intuition, wisdom, and immense generosity.

Enocha Ranjita Ryan, for her loving, healing friendship, her unwavering belief in me, and her deep love of God that nourishes everyone around her.

Debra Light, for being a soul sister with practical advice, abundant love, unending encouragement, and intuitive support.

Marci Matthews, for intuitive readings, endless hospitality, and her ageless spirit.

Wayan Kartini, for her TLC in Bali and beyond.

Lili Shadab, soul sister, tech goddess, for her design advice, sweet spirit, inner strength, and "sacred getaways."

Barbara Tira, for insightful Body Harmony, Family Constellations and loving kindness.

LoOuita Daniel, 95 years young and still interested, able and independent.

Gwen Gordon, amazing artist, graphic designer and friend who so generously helped me.

Cathy Lehman, photographer, friend and sweet neighbor to my mom.

I am so truly blessed by dear friends and family who hold me in the Light of God and who inspire and uplift me every day. You are all MAPS (Motivation And Power Sources) for me.

♥   ♥   ♥

So many blessings. Thank you.

Introduction

This journey began for me in 2006 when I was living in Nyuh Kuning, a small village just outside of the town of Ubud, in Bali, Indonesia. I noticed that my morning meditations were becoming filled with information about MAPS: what they are, how to identify them, how to make and to use them, and their potential for change. I was very specifically receiving knowledge of what motivation and power sources is all about.

I realized that I was being given guidance and direction to bring this material into physical manifestation. In other words, I was being asked to write a guidebook showing others how to create and to use this powerful self-help tool to change their thinking, enhance their confidence and self-esteem and, most of all, to be in the present moment, the conscious *now* where their true power resides.

Because I have a strong commitment to listen to my Higher (Inner) Guidance and follow It's direction, I agreed to follow through and write the information as it was given to me. From there, the process and this guidebook began. There is nothing new about the ideas, but perhaps these are new ways of looking at and utilizing what's available to us.

I returned to California in August of that year because my mother had fallen and broken her knee. I went to take care of her, and during her recovery, I began creating some MAPS for her and other family members and friends.

I soon realized that I needed to make them for myself as well, and to find a book that I could keep them in that was also small enough for me to carry and to access at all times. I was constantly being reminded to have them with me so they would be available when I needed them.

When my mother was better, I went to visit my dear friend Linda and shared with her all of the information that I had received. We went about finding a book and began creating them together. It worked perfectly.

I couldn't stop making MAPS and immediately understood their purpose. Each one, even the most basic and least creative, was motivating and empowering to me. I was thinking about them all the time and discovering more every day. I was being given the realization that motivation and power sources were everywhere, just waiting to be identified and discovered, and to bring me into the present *now* awareness. I was experiencing the profound positive effect they had on me.

I also kept noticing how specific people, places, activities, and things were motivation and power sources for me. I could see how doing things that I loved and enjoyed kept me in the present moment and motivated and empowered me to make better choices and take more positive action.

I could see that MAPS are everywhere, and that we've all had motivation and power sources with us throughout our lives. A teddy bear, a blanket, a special shell found at the ocean, a person who always makes us feel good, an inspirational phrase from a song or a book—these are motivation and power sources because they have special meaning and value to us.

Throughout our lives, we grow up identifying things that have special meanings. Things that uplift, inspire, and make us feel good when we see them and connect with them are motivation and power sources for us. We may keep them in a special place—on an altar, in our room, home, car, or workspace—or carry them with us in a book, a backpack, a purse, a pouch, or on our smartphone, computer, or other device.

I also could see that the concept of MAPS was the container for all of the things that I had discovered, created, and identified as personal motivation and power sources throughout my life. All of the inspirational quotes, all the words, phrases, and pictures that I'd gathered over the years, or just found today, were MAPS to the present moment. All the little talismans and sacred objects that I had carried for years took on new and revitalized meanings.

I began doing workshops to share the concept and process with others, including friends and family. Linda also began sharing it with some of her friends, coworkers, and students.

I returned to Bali and shared MAPS with friends there. Being open and receptive to Higher Guidance, more information was given to me. I was experiencing the energetic impact and I received positive feedback about how others were experiencing their MAPS as well.

When I came back to California just before Christmas, 2007, I was diagnosed with breast cancer. I realized that this was an invitation to really test all of this on an even deeper level.

Not only did MAPS prove to be an important part of my journey through the disease, I also witnessed and experienced their profound strengthening and healing power and their ability to change fear and doubt into confidence and certainty, worry and darkness to faith and light.

I'll never forget the day that I had a real meltdown. I couldn't stop crying and just wanted a day off from cancer. My youngest son arrived with flowers, balloons, and a teddy bear. Needless to say, that teddy bear is a motivation and power source for me, and to this day, he sits in my car and rides with me everywhere. Just looking at him always puts a smile on my face.

My MAPS brought me through the recovery of surgery and radiation, and they have proven to be an ongoing source of creativity, fun, and inspiration. The workshops that I have done with other cancer patients have been received with much enthusiasm and validation of how beneficial they are.

I love MAPS because they never fail to uplift me, make me feel good, and bring me into present power. The more time and energy I invest in them, the greater the benefits I receive.

When I returned to Bali after radiation in July, 2008, more information was given to me. What had started out as a handout a few pages long about what MAPS are and how to make them was becoming more detailed information about how they can be used for changing thoughts, moods, beliefs, and behaviors.

I remember being in Lovina, on the northwest shore of Bali, receiving the Altars, Alters, and Music chapter and feeling so grateful for it and the blessed life that I live. I had thought at the time that it was the final bit, but Spirit (Guidance) let me know that it wasn't quite complete. There was quite a bit more to come.

I moved back to California in September of 2009. I continued working with the MAPS, doing small group and private sessions, receiving more guidance about them, making additions and edits, and occasionally stepping back to let it all sink in. I've spent much time living the concepts and utilizing all the material.

It is now summer, 2014, and I am finally finishing the details of this guidebook. Technology MAPS, of course, had to be included. Divine timing is always the determining factor. I'm now feeling that this is just about ready to be published. But of course, I am open to the possibility of more, since Infinite Source always has the final word.

This has been a most interesting journey for me, and it continues to evolve. As the concept has developed, I have found that the more I use MAPS, make them, and share them with others, the more energetically enhanced they are.

As the Law of Attraction works, more and more inspiration comes. I wake up thinking about MAPS, and throughout the day, more ideas and actual motivation and power sources reveal themselves to me.

I see MAPS all around me wherever I go. The morning light on the mountains, the rose in the vase on my desk, the hummingbird in my garden have always been sources of inspiration for me. What is ordinary becomes extraordinary. What is already beautiful takes on a quality of the sacred and divine.

I find "the committee" convening less and less often, and when it does, it's easy to get back on track to thinking and feeling good and quickly moving away from doubt, worry, and fear. The negative committee members (critics, judges, etc.) are replaced with positive members (cheerleaders and coaches) who encourage me with "Yes you can!" "You go, girl!" and "Good on you!"

My motivation and power sources actually change my mind and change my mood. Remember that when we change our perception, we change our experience. I feel better, inspired, and energized. I feel motivated and empowered.

Identifying, discovering, and making MAPS is fun. It is creative expression without any need for talent or training. Anyone can do it and benefit from them because in the process, we are in the present moment, focused on the positive. We are creating and designing our future.

I am so excited to be sharing all of this with you. I trust that as you discover MAPS, define them, make your own, and refer to them often, you will see noticeable positive differences in the way that you feel and the way you experience your life.

So when you hit a bump, get to your MAPS. They are the "thrive-all" kit with everything you need to move forward, feel better, and be your best. They are the internal GPS that is your personal roadmap from your little self to your greater Self.

♥   ♥   ♥

"Like the moon,
Come out from behind the clouds!
And Shine."

—Buddha

Boundless blessings and love,
Sande

Chapter 1

What are MAPS to the Present Moment?

Motivation and power sources are MAPS. The standard definitions are as follows:

- Motivation means to be stimulated to action. It's an impulse to action that determines our choices or moves our will.
- Power is a means of supplying energy to change an action, thought, mood, or behavior. It's any form of energy available for doing something.
- A source is the cause or origin of something, anything that provides inspiration for action. It's the place where something begins, where it springs into being.

MAPS are any person, place, word, quote, phrase, picture, music, sound, action, activity, or thing that brings you into *present moment consciousness* and inspires you to feel motivated and empowered to think, feel, and act more positively.

MAPS shift one's state of feeling to a higher frequency and optimal state for manifesting change. They are self-empowerment tools that work to enhance self-esteem, confidence, and one's ability to take positive action when faced with negative thinking and unwanted feelings or moods.

Simply put, MAPS are your internal GPS, guiding you up when you're down, moving you from confusion to clarity, and getting you out of a stuck position to take positive action. They do this by bringing you into the *present moment*, where choice and change can take place.

Your personal MAPS are anything, anyone, any place that brings *you* into the present moment (*now* consciousness) and changes the way you're thinking and feeling.

They are your personal sources of inspiration which provide the energy to stimulate an internal impulse to think and feel better.

Chapter 2

Applications

MAPS have many applications because of their ability to influence our thoughts and feelings, alter our perceptions, build our self-esteem, and enhance our confidence. Their ability to motivate and empower us contributes to the energy required to inspire action.

As a self-help tool, they are very effective in overcoming negative thought patterns and beliefs that no longer serve us. They help us create new ways of thinking that are both uplifting and creative, and they open our hearts and minds to new possibilities.

I have also found MAPS to be extremely healing. They have become an important part of my journey through breast cancer. I continue to be profoundly impacted by their energy medicine. I believe this energy to be a big part of my recovery and the restoration of my health, wholeness, and well-being.

These are ways that MAPS can be used:

- for personal self-empowerment
- to change disempowering thoughts, feelings, moods, beliefs, or behaviors
- to inspire and uplift yourself and others
- as parent-and-child activities

- as classroom activities
- as activities for small group gatherings and sessions with friends
- as an aid to healing disease, illness, or depression
- as altars
- for stress relief
- to enhance your gratitude and appreciation
- to bring you into more conscious awareness
- to enhance awareness of yourself and others
- for fun and creative self-expression

Use your imagination for more possibilities of how MAPS can be used to help you.

Chapter 3

General Information about MAPS

We want to feel inspired, uplift ourselves, overcome negative thinking, and be motivated to take positive action. We want to find that place within that empowers us to live our best life, through the ups and downs. MAPS give us a direction to follow; they guide us and show us the way to a desired destination. They bring us into the present moment, where awareness and choice are available.

The MAPS spoken of here are specifically for self-empowerment and conscious awareness. They help us remember who we truly are. They remind us that we have choices and inspire us to be the best we can be and feel the best we can feel.

We are constantly challenged by other people, circumstances, and situations to think positively, see obstacles and challenges as opportunities, and respond from a higher, wiser place within ourselves.

We are bombarded with distractions from external sources like the media, traffic, noises, etc. Internal forces like illnesses, long-held emotional issues and beliefs that no longer serve our greatest good, and fear in various forms such as doubt, anger, and guilt also keep us distracted. Our brains like to analyze things and get carried away.

We all have what I call a "committee." These are the voices in our heads, the self-talk. This committee holds board meetings at the drop of a hat.

Its members taunt us night and day, rain or shine, for no apparent reason other than to set us back, break us down, elicit doubt, and generally make us feel bad.

This committee is extremely judgmental. It says things like, "What's wrong with you?", "You can't do that.", "You're too fat, too thin, too slow.", "What makes you think you deserve that?" And on and on and on until we are disabled with doubt, fear, discouragement, and more.

The result is our feeling unmotivated, uninspired, and lacking the energy and enthusiasm to go after our dreams or to follow through on the simplest project or desire.

This committee is not necessarily bad. It is just made up of wounded, fractured parts of us and past experiences that represent fear. Fear takes numerous forms, including these committee members who are angry, judgmental naysayers. Giving them limited time to speak and acknowledging their needs with loving kindness is important in self-healing. I do believe we must be gentle with ourselves, so perhaps allow a few minutes here and there to hear their grievances and then let them know that the board meeting is postponed. Sorry, enough complaints for one day, week, month, or year!

Let's keep postponing these board meetings. Kindly dismiss the committee, and every time they reconvene, dismiss them again and again and again with positive alternatives. Your MAPS will do just that because they will motivate you and give you the power to change your thinking easily and quickly. They will be ongoing sources of inspiration and motivation to take the action needed to change what you want and need to change.

Your MAPS are very personal tools specific to you and your needs, wants, and desires. You choose, you decide, and you create exactly what is right for you to feel motivated and empowered anytime, anywhere.

MAPS literally guide us and show us the way to reconnect continually with that place within that knows anything is possible and we can do it. They give us the direction and focus to turn our thinking into energy that can create the positive outcomes we want in our lives, be they health and well-being, or abundance and prosperity.

It is often said, "What we think about, we bring about," and "Where attention goes, energy flows." The more we can redirect our thoughts to good, better, best, the more we experience good, better, best.

Your personal MAPS are with you at all times to use whenever you need them. They are a powerful ally to keep you in the present, where your power is. They will guide you to where you want to go, to who you want to be, and to how you want to live your life.

Here's a little rhyme to illustrate how annoying and debilitating negative thinking can be!

The Committee

These judges, these critics
Are driving me mad.
Their meetings are endless,
Their harassment so bad.

I want them to shut up,
Cease all conversation.
Give me a break;
I need relaxation.

I've tried to ignore them,
Swam the river Denial.
Where's the relief?
Can't they stop for a while?

Slamming and spewing
Every negative label,
Can't even one of them
Just leave the table?

Incessant, persistent,
They keep on berating.
I've canceled each meeting,
But they're not relating.

No mercy they show me.
What is their story?
They're hell-bent on seeing
That I have no glory.

I must end this badgering
With uplifted thinking
Before it's too late,
Or this boat is sinking.

Why won't they let
The cheerleaders meet
To give me some help,
Get me back on my feet?

I just need some positives,
Good energy flow;
Some strong affirmations
Could help me, I know.

Yet just when I think
I have the committee dismissed,
They start in again,
With their snakelike *hiss hiss*.

You're this or you're that,
Why can't you, what's wrong?
Their labels and judgments
Are a horrible song.

These monsters are brutal,
Overtaking my brain.
Their negative chatter
Nearly drives me insane.

Why can't I get rid of them
Once and for all?
Stand straight and strong,
Prepared not to fall.

My God, oh my angels,
Please help me, I plead.
Stop this nasty committee,
So I can succeed.

Give me the power,
The confidence and will
To stop all these critics
And make them be still.

Change "down" thoughts to "up" thoughts,
Dear Lord, I do pray.
Right now in this moment,
I need a good day.

If I don't get busy
And just learn the trick
To keep them away,
I'll surely be sick.

If health goes, I'm really
Asking for trouble,
'Cause that old committee
Will meet on the double.

They'll use every symptom,
They'll push me to fall,
Convince me of weakness
That's not true at all.

MAPS: a solution
So simple, it's clear.
When making and using,
I'm present, I'm here.

My thoughts, they are shifting
From bottom to top.
I find the direction—
The committee now stops!

Right in the *now*,
Where power is real,
Tap into the Source;
I know it, I feel.

Brain research has shown us that the two hemispheres of our brain function differently. The left hemisphere focuses on linear thinking, the past and the future. It thinks in language and calculations. It is the inner voice saying *I am separate*. The left hemisphere is where the brain chatter (the committee) emanates from.

The right hemisphere is all about the present moment. It thinks in pictures. The imagination can run wild. The right hemisphere encompasses a larger, open view which conceptualizes holistically and it is where our creative thinking emerges from.

Our goal is to increase the communication between the hemispheres and create new neural pathways, bringing balance and synchronicity. As the hemispheres become more and more synchronized, we are more able to reduce the mind chatter and focus our attention.

MAPS are constantly helping us to stay in present moment consciousness so that we can come into the fullest and highest expression of ourselves.

For freedom from mental suffering (the committee), find your MAPS to:

- be grateful;
- stop judging yourself and others;
- forgive yourself and others;
- be kind to yourself and others; and
- smile and laugh often.

Chapter 4

The Present Power of MAPS

The present moment is the only place from which you can change your thoughts, feelings, and perceptions. It is where awareness and conscious choice live. The present moment, the conscious *now*, is the only place from where you can clearly set intentions for your life, your goals, and your future. MAPS are a powerful tool because they continually bring you back to the present, where all of your power resides.

These MAPS (words, pictures, objects, people, sounds, music, places, actions, etc.) are your connection to the motivation and power that you need to move from here to there, from a negative thought to a positive thought, from a bad feeling to a good or better feeling, from being stuck to taking conscious action.

Think about something or someone who always uplifts you, makes you feel good. They are sources of motivation and power to you. You think about them and immediately are in a better place mentally, inspired to take positive action.

Your motivation and power sources are what bring you to conscious awareness in the present moment. Now you can change the definition of things and circumstances so that your experience of them can be perceived as a gift, an opportunity, or a lesson to be learned instead of a problem, a crisis, or a drama to be overcome.

Some of the MAPS that you can make are similar to vision boards and scrapbooking, as they use words and pictures in a creative way. Vision boards are a very powerful way to influence your future, and scrapbooking is a beautiful and fun way to remember the past. Journaling is also an important and useful way to record the past and set intentions for the future. I have used journaling and vision boards throughout the years with extremely helpful and often wonderful results.

If you think of vision boards as designating a future goal, then MAPS are the motivation and power sources that get you to that goal. Successfully accomplishing any goal requires positive thinking, feeling, and action *in the present.*

Vision boards are powerful MAPS. Looking at or thinking about your vision board changes how you feel in the moment, uplifts your thinking, and inspires insight into actions that will lead you to your goal. Vision boards motivate and empower you to make better choices and take positive action—now, in the present moment. These are the choices and actions that help us achieve our goals.

The intention of MAPS is purely to motivate and empower you—in the present moment—to make necessary changes in your thoughts, moods, feelings, and actions. They are the energy tools to help you to think better thoughts, feel better about yourself, and take the best action to ensure your best outcomes. They are virtually and literally a map, directions, your internal GPS, and the way to where you want to go. When you're down, go up; when you're lost, find your way; when you're confused, get clarity. This is what MAPS do for you.

When MAPS started coming to me and I began working with them myself and with others, I realized immediately what a powerful tool for change and for good they are. I saw that every time I used them, without fail, I was brought to the present, immensely inspired and greatly energized. What fun it has been to see something so simple and easy be so dynamic and have such profound results.

Whenever my committee starts up, I go to my MAPS and immediately change the direction of my thinking. When I find myself complaining or notice that I have lost conscious awareness, I go to my MAPS and get present, aware, and able to choose a better thought or action.

When I was diagnosed with breast cancer in December 2007, I realized this was a perfect opportunity to really test these MAPS. It was a chance for me to see if and how they would work as I traveled the road to health and wholeness. I was challenged every day to open my heart and mind to the infinite possibilities that life has to offer.

I can tell you unequivocally that MAPS have been and continue to be a vital and necessary part of my journey. They always bring me out of any fear, doubt, or worry that tries to hold me back or bring me down.

I invite you to discover, gather, and make your MAPS and to let them be the motivation and power sources that will help you live a healthy, happy, fulfilling life. Intuition, creativity, insight, and realization come from and into the present moment, often with profound results in the future.

"The inner alignment with NOW is the end of suffering."

—Eckhart Tolle, *Stillness Speaks*

Chapter 5

How MAPS Work

Think about maps in the traditional sense. They are literally pictures with words and names of destinations showing you how to get from one place to another. They give you the direct routes to any destination. When you're lost, confused, or don't know the way, they give you the directions you need to get from where you are to where you want to go.

MAPS (motivation and power sources) do the very same thing. They get you from one place to another inwardly. So when you're lost, stuck, or confused, they head you in the right direction like a GPS. They give you the guidance to find your way. They get you out of your stuck position and give you the clarity to escape your confusion. They give you the motivation and power to change your thinking, clear your mind, and get moving in a more positive direction.

MAPS work energetically. They are the very sources that personally motivate and empower you. They are things that you have identified, discovered, or created and can be used whenever you need them.

What good is any map if you don't have it with you when you need it? That is why you want to always have your MAPS with you and around you. Make sure they are accessible to you at all times, whenever you want or need them. Have them in your room, home, workplace, car, purse, wallet, pocket, and on your computer, iPad, smartphone, etc. Know to whom and where you can go to for inspiration and support when you need it.

Here are some examples:

You get up in the morning and go about starting your day, getting ready for an appointment with your boss. You then notice (become aware) that your committee is holding a board meeting. Kindly cancel; dismiss it and get to your MAPS: the affirmation taped to your bathroom mirror, the song on your iPod. Your MAPS immediately bring you into the present moment, where you are reminded of who you truly are (a spiritual being in a physical body). They remind you of what you want and how you want to feel. They give you the inspiration, motivation, and power to change your thinking in a more positive direction so you can get back to being the best you can be. Okay, now you're ready for the world.

The appointment goes well and you sail along, feeling good, thinking good thoughts—until a coworker says or does something that annoys you. Oh, now the committee has reconvened and they are in full swing. Kindly cancel, dismiss them, again!

You already have MAPS with you, in your office, your pocket, your smartphone, your mind. Remember, you've always got some MAPS with you and around you. Just thinking about them makes them energetically work for you, bringing you to present-moment awareness. Instantly, you are inspired to react or respond more positively. Your MAPS have guided you back on track to how you want to feel and experience your day.

Our thoughts, feelings, words, and actions are always creating our future. Remember: "What we think about, we bring about," and "Where attention goes, energy flows." Having your MAPS with you and accessible at all times will give you the security of knowing that, in any given situation, they will be there for you to direct you, guide you, in the most positive direction.

By looking at your MAPS, thinking about them, and even touching them, you are actually drawing energy from them to change your thinking and focus. They are truly sources of motivation and power that will continually uplift and inspire you. The more you think positive, good thoughts and feel good feelings, the more you create the future you desire.

The science of neuroplasticity is revealing the brain's ability to reorganize itself when we form new neuron connections throughout life. This explains how MAPS affect and even change our brains. Whenever we do something different in order to interrupt a set behavior or thought pattern, we are literally connecting synapses in the brain that eventually rewire, changing the old into new.

By utilizing both the left and right hemispheres of the brain, we are creating new thoughts, behaviors, and habits and building neuron connections that eventually produce desired outcomes. You are creating something different from what you've grown used to in your personal world and changing the way you routinely think and feel each day.

Another extremely important element is our perception and how we define things. To change our perception is to change our experience. We can redefine anything so that our experience of it will be positive, enriching, and empowering.

I used to be intimidated by and resistant to computers. I defined them as complex, frustrating, and confusing, being unwilling to get familiar with them. Then I got a laptop—I knew I had to change my mind about it or return it quickly and not get involved.

I decided to give computers a new meaning for myself; they could be a challenge, an opportunity to learn something new, to stimulate my brain and have fun with it. With that, I felt motivated to take some classes and play around with this new little gadget and see what we could do together.

By changing my perception and how I defined the computer, I began to have a whole new experience. The intimidation was gone, and I began seeing this little technological wonder as something fun and helpful.

We give definitions and meaning to everything. We perceive what others say, what they do, and what situations we're in as either positive or negative, whether it pleases us or not. These personal perceptions (our definitions, our meanings) determine our experience of what is said, what is done, and what is, in any given moment. It is vital that we continually redefine (give new meaning) to words, actions, events, and situations. By doing this, we can change how we think, feel, and experience anything.

Give things the most positive definitions you can to make your life experiences as good as they can be and to have the most positive outcomes. Even the most difficult situation can be perceived as an opportunity, a gift, or a lesson that makes you better than you were before. You choose; you decide how you want to feel about anything.

Some of your MAPS can be in a book, an envelope, a bag, a pouch, on your smartphone, iPad, etc. They can be pictures, words, talismans, sacred objects, or music—anything that you define as meaningful, inspirational, motivating, empowering, and uplifting. They will work for you because that is your intention.

Think about a sacred object or a special piece of jewelry which, when you touch it, immediately makes you feel centered, clear, safe, and empowered. I have a ring I wear that brings me present immediately when I touch it or look at it. Someone else might have a necklace or stone they hold on to when they feel afraid or anxious and brings them back to a sense of "I'm ok, I can do this."

Identify and discover what your motivation and power sources are. Make MAPS and refer to them often. The process of making MAPS is itself a source of motivation and power, and referring to them later is motivating and empowering as well. It's important that you have them with you and around you all the time, whenever you need them. I have friends and family I call upon who are sources of motivation, places that I go to for inspiration, and books that contain messages of empowerment. When I can't sleep, I have several CDs that I can play and in no time, I'm back asleep again.

Some of your MAPS will change over time and at different times in your life. What may have motivated and inspired you in the past could be different now and in the future. You will find that you are continually identifying, discovering, collecting, and creating new ones.

The Create to Integrate worksheets throughout this guidebook are a great beginning and resource to refer to and continually add to. Refer to these lists when you need to shift your internal energy. Just thinking about any one of your MAPS will move you in the direction you want to go.

MAPS to the present moment are like exercise, (but a lot more fun): the more you put into it, the more you get out of it.

"Choosing the path of wisdom,
become aware of those things which lead you forward
and those which hold you back."

—Buddha

Chapter 6

Who, Where, What MAPS

Many wise ones have said, "The company you keep is stronger than your will." This means that the people, places, and situations that we surround ourselves with have an influence on our lives. These influences can affect our thinking, our moods, our feelings, and our behaviors.

When we are around people who gossip, complain, use harsh language, or judge and criticize others, we sometimes can find ourselves joining in and/or feeling uncomfortable in their company.

People who are positive and grateful, see the best in others, and appreciate the blessings they have are the ones who inspire us to be better. These are the people it feels good to be with because they are motivation and power sources. They don't dwell in the past, complain, or judge themselves or others. They are positive and enthusiastic about life.

It feels good to be around people who are happy, who live their lives with a positive attitude, who see the possibilities through the problems, and who take positive action to make things better for themselves and everyone around them. These are the people to spend more time with; you can enjoy their company and the positive energy that surrounds them.

There are places we go that feel dark, depressing, or just uncomfortable in some way or other. Even a room can affect us negatively if it's not clean, or if it's cluttered, messy, or dark. Beautiful places, cheerful, calm, peaceful environments, can soothe us and inspire us to be clearer, more centered, energized, and relaxed. These places are motivation and power sources for us.

It always feels good to be nurtured by nature and to be in beautiful surroundings. Nature and beauty have a way of soothing our souls. Spending time at the ocean, in the mountains, or at any beautiful natural setting can easily change how we're feeling and thinking. A day at the museum or at the botanical gardens can do wonders to inspire you. Find your special places and spend more time there.

The situations in which we put ourselves or find ourselves also have an influence on how we feel. Too much media news can be disturbing, depressing, even scary. Listening to or talking about all the bad and negative things that are happening in our city, in our country, or in the world can give us cause to feel less hopeful or optimistic.

Situations that are considered motivation and power sources are ones that make us feel good, that empower us to think positively, and that energize us to take positive action. Hang out with uplifting people and have conversations about what's working and what can make the world a better place. Spend time playing with your children or pets. Create situations that uplift you.

Going to classes, workshops, seminars, groups, or meetings where you feel inspired and learn new ways to be your best can be MAPS to the present moment. Movies, music, concerts, and plays are inspirational and uplifting MAPS as well. If I'm stuck in traffic, I have inspiring motivational CDs to keep me calm and my thoughts positive.

Everything has a positive, neutral, or negative effect that is subtle or profound. A day at the ocean, a beautiful sunset, kind and loving words from a friend, the birth of a baby, hurtful criticism from a coworker, a traffic jam, a canceled date, a death—all are interpreted in one way or another.

Do you see obstacles as challenges or as opportunities? Do you feel cursed or blessed? Do you see what's wrong and complain, or do you see what's right and what's working? Do you blame or do you take responsibility? Do you dwell in the past or future instead of in the now? Do you get stuck in the problems or explore the possibilities? Do you make excuses or do you take positive action?

Identify the people, places, and situations that are motivation and power sources for you and spend much more time with and in them so that you will be inspired and energized to be your best and feel your best.

Create a positive environment in your home, room, or workplace by adding objects that are MAPS, such as fresh flowers, plants, and art. Hang out with people who are cheerful, positive, possibility thinkers, problem solvers. Go to places that uplift you and help you come back renewed, recharged, and revitalized. A short time at the ocean can change my mood in a minute.

Discover and identify what works for you. Any person, place, situation, or thing can be a source of motivation and power for you if it brings you into present-moment consciousness, makes you feel better, and inspires you to be better.

The world needs all of us to be the best we can be. We can all add more light and positive energy to it, which will diminish the darkness, hatred, and fear. You make a difference. Be a source of motivation and power for someone else.

"Look carefully around you and recognize the luminosity of souls. Sit beside those who draw you to that."

—Rumi

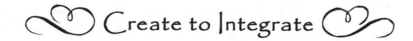
Create to Integrate

Make a list of at least five people, places, situations, and things that are MAPS for you.

People: These can be people you personally know or don't know, living or dead, who make you feel good and inspire or motivate you when you see them, talk with them, or think of them.

_____

_____

_____

_____

Places: These are places that always make you feel good when you go there or think about them; they are places that inspire, motivate, or empower you.

_____

_____

_____

_____

Situations: These are situations that always make you feel good, cheer you up, and inspire, motivate, or empower you. (Examples: lunch out with a special friend, a great massage, a workshop, playing with your dog or cat.)

_____

_____

_____

_____

Things: These are things that are a source of inspiration, motivation, and power for you and make you feel good when you see, hear, or touch them. (Examples: a special piece of jewelry, a book, a song, a bouquet of fresh flowers, your pet, a special crystal.)

_____

_____

_____

_____

Keep adding to these lists and refer to them often.

Chapter 7

Technology MAPS

So many of us now have access to computers, smartphones, Kindles, iPods, iPads, etc. What wonderful gadgets in our homes, offices and hands so we can have MAPS with us at all times. In an instant, we can find something to laugh about, to make us smile, to stir our compassion, and to make ourselves and each other feel better than we did a minute ago.

And it goes without saying, though I will anyway, that nearly every day, something new, updated, improved, and more amazing is offered to us—and this will continue to happen. Technology is moving at warp speed.

Think of the sites you can visit to get information about anything you are interested in. You can get motivated and inspired by a myriad of ideas, people, places, and things. There are endless things to see and hear for fun and laughter and information and inspiration.

We have to constantly remind ourselves that an excess of anything is out of balance. Total absorption in these devices is counterproductive to our being our best selves and living our best lives. Our interactions with one another and with the natural world are the keys to experiencing a healthy, happy, fulfilling life. Utilize technology for your greatest good and that of others.

Spend some time on the positive sites and steer clear of the negative ones. Use social media sites to motivate and empower yourself and each other.

Stay away from the haters and cyber bullies. Find the sites and sources that help you to be your best and a positive influence on others.

The joy of instantaneously sharing a photo with a distant friend or relative and that great email from a loved one just when you were missing him or her are just a couple of the ways we can be touched and moved by what these technological devices offer us.

We must be vigilant, knowing that there is as much potential for darkness as there is for light.

I often find meaningful quotes, great pictures, and videos on the internet that are uplifting and remind me of the positive direction I always want to move in. A friend told me recently about a device she wears that calculates steps walked and health goals met and alerts her with positive feedback as she achieves the goals she sets for herself.

Connect with the MAPS (motivation and power sources) that are meaningful to you, the ones that bring you into the present in a positive way and inspire you to think and feel uplifted and energized. Connect with what helps you make the best choices and decisions for yourself and others and empowers you to be your best. So many things are available to us, and new ones arrive every day.

Support the sites and social media that have a positive impact and inspire positive change. Pinterest is a good place to find beautiful photos of anything you love and enjoy, from puppies to penguins, butterflies to beaches, fashion to flowers, or whatever else are MAPS for you. You can find funny quotes to laugh at or wisdom to live by. There are unlimited sources of motivation and power to be discovered if you just look in the right places.

Inspiration and insight can be found with very little time and effort, and many causes, charities, and volunteer opportunities based on your interests and availability are just waiting for you. The internet is a great place to find MAPS and share them with others.

♥   ♥   ♥

"Life has a bright side and a dark side, for the world of relativity
is composed of light and shadows....Look only for the good
in everything, that you absorb the quality of beauty."

—Paramahansa Yogananda, *Where There Is Light*

❤ Create to Integrate ❤

What technological devices do you own and use (a computer, a smartphone, etc.) that can give you access to MAPS to the present moment?

_____

_____

_____

What are some of the websites that you feel are sources of motivation and power for you? List sites that make you smile, that inspire you, and that uplift you when you're down, or remind you of your potential.

_____

_____

_____

_____

_____

This can get you started on thinking about all the positive possibilities that technology has to offer.

Chapter 8

Altars, Alters, and Music

An altar is a special, designated place where sacred objects, pictures, photos, figures, talismans, etc. are placed and where prayers and offerings are made to honor, bless and give thanks for blessings received.

To alter something means to change, modify, or transform it in some way. To alter one's perception would be to change it, to see things differently than before the alteration took place.

I have been guided to discover and realize that MAPS can both be *altars* and *alter* my thinking.

I see now that some things I've been doing for many years have been and still are MAPS for me. My altars hold photos, figures, special stones and crystals—objects that are special or sacred to me. All of the things on my altars are truly motivation and power sources.

When I travel, I can open one of my MAPS books, prop it up on a table or dresser, and have an instant altar before me, continually altering my thoughts and feelings. They always bring me to a state of feeling grateful, blessed, inspired, and motivated to live in the present moment with an open heart and mind.

MAPS constantly alter my perceptions, thoughts, and feelings. In the morning, they empower me to move into and through the day with good, positive energy, and at night, before sleep, they remind me of who I really am and of the Infinite Source of all the good that comes into my life. MAPS are not themselves the Infinite Source, but they do come from the Infinite Source of All That Is.

I have always carried with me special little objects that have significance and power. Like the talismans and sacred objects in the medicine pouch of a Native American shaman, these things motivate and empower me. By touching them or looking at them I am brought back into the powerful present-moment *now* consciousness.

When I work with divination cards, like Native American Medicine cards, Angel cards, Sacred Geometry cards, I often write down the messages received and even put the card on my altar for the day. Certain cards have special significance and are particularly timely and profoundly insightful. These cards and their messages often serve as MAPS for me.

You can create small altars in your home, room, car, garden, workspace, etc. by putting objects and pictures where you can see them often. See how focusing on your altar alters your thoughts, feelings, and moods. Notice how these MAPS are altering your thinking and bringing you into the present moment, uplifting, motivating, and inspiring you.

I find that when I look at the little altars I have created, I am reminded of how blessed and grateful I am for my divine connection to Spirit, God, All That Is. Every time I look at them, I am brought to the present moment, feeling the love, support, and protection that surround me in the visible and invisible worlds. I become centered and clear in the now consciousness of my life, where peace and gratitude are alive in me. Create an altar for yourself and see how it alters you.

When it comes to altering a mood or attitude, music is also a dynamic source of motivation and power. When the lyrics are positive and inspirational, they alter my thoughts and feelings. Who doesn't feel better listening to an uplifting or beautiful piece of music? If it makes you feel like dancing in your seat or up on our feet, that's great. But if it touches your heart and soul, even better. I always have music MAPS with me, especially in the car!

As you can see, MAPS are everywhere, already waiting for you to pick and choose what motivates and empowers you. Infinite Source, All That Is, God, Divine Principle offers everything you need to be inspired to live your happiest, healthiest, most fulfilling life.

♥   ♥   ♥

"In the future, in the distance, those are illusions.
Taste the here and now of God."

—Rumi

༼ Create to Integrate ༽

1. Find a place where you can create an altar. Use anything that appeals to you. Shells, stones, sticks, feathers, crystals, flowers, and photos are all good examples. Use whatever is special to you. Pay attention to what you're choosing and how the process of creating your altar makes you feel. Take some time to write about your process and your feelings. Record anything that has been altered in your perception about altars.

_____

_____

_____

_____

2. List some music that is a source of motivation and power to you: your music MAPS.

_____

_____

_____

_____

Chapter 9

Rituals, Routines, and Practices

The other day, one of my sons said to me that it seems like every day we have to create our own happiness. Like carving it out and sculpting it with a pickax. He told me that's what his morning routine does. He sits in the tub and just lets everything go, relaxes, and affirms: I am divinely guided, protected, and directed. Opportunity flows to me easily and effortlessly. He refers to these five to ten minutes in the bath or shower as a time to go through a series of words and images that motivate him to go out and be in the world in an empowered way. Another son uses the time before sleep to read, reflect and prepare his mind and spirit for the next day.

They reminded me of the power of ritual and routine. I began reflecting on the rituals and routines that I have participated in and ones that I've created throughout my life. I know what an incredible mechanism they are for centering and grounding and how helpful they are for uplifting and energizing me. They are also a very powerful way to be in the present moment, in the dynamic *now* where inspiration and insight come from.

These daily routines, rituals, and practices work so inconspicuously that we may not notice the profound and beneficial impact they have on us. We may see and feel their importance more when we are faced with a challenge or confronted with our own or someone else's stressful emotions. Yet these daily rituals and routines are the very things that get us started, keep us going, calm us down, lift our spirits, and send us off to a good night's sleep.

Our daily rituals, routines, and practices are openings to a deeper understanding of ourselves, to insights and realizations, and they turn out to be very useful destressors. They truly are motivation and power sources.

Here is a small list of rituals, routines, and practices that I have found to be extremely beneficial over the years: meditation, mantras, mudras, energization exercises, walking, yoga, breathing exercises, affirmations, chanting, and visualizations. Any practice of recognizing and honoring blessings and seeing the sacred and divine in your life is a benefit beyond measure.

Lighting candles and creating an atmosphere of peaceful receptivity can be another way of centering and allowing our Higher Guidance to come through. These rituals, routines, and practices are where we can dive deeper, slow down, and listen to our souls calling. There is an inner longing in all of us to make the shift from a human doing to a human being.

We spend so much of our time living on the surface, dealing with what's in front of us in a somewhat disconnected way. We text instead of talking, shoot off quick emails instead of thoughtful, handwritten letters, eat food on the run instead of sitting down to family dinners. We rush from this meeting to that to get everyone to school and work on time. These are some of the ways a fast pace keeps us distracted and wanting more out of life.

See what rituals, routines, and practices you can find and develop for yourself. Do them daily to enhance your ability to be content, to feel peace in your heart and mind, and to experience well-being in your body, mind, and soul.

Remember, our brains are always growing new neuron connections, and new practices will create new ways of thinking and being.

When you add these rituals, routines, and practices to all of the other MAPS you have discovered, identified, and created, you will truly have a "thrive-all kit" that will serve you well in any circumstance or condition. Your MAPS are your way through tough times, and they make the good times even better.

♥   ♥   ♥

"Meditation, or any solitary practice, (a walk before dawn, a poem every morning, sitting on the roof at sunset) gives depth and expands the souls action...Anything you do every day can open into the deepest spiritual place, which is freedom."

—Coleman Barks, *The Essential Rumi*

 Create to Integrate

Take a few minutes to think about routines, rituals, and practices that you do which help you to stay centered and have a positive influence on your thoughts and feelings.

Some examples are daily meditations, morning or evening walks, a bath with candles and soft music, yoga practice, and playing a musical instrument. Anything you do on a regular basis that is a source of motivation and power can be listed here.

Write down at least three daily rituals, routines, or practices that you do or that you can do to feel motivated and empowered and which bring you into the present and help you think and feel better.

_____

_____

_____

How do these rituals, routines, or practices influence or change your thoughts?

_____

_____

_____

After doing the rituals, routines, or practices you have listed, how do you feel?

_____

_____

_____

Chapter 10

Gratitude and Service MAPS

I believe the most powerful sources of motivation and power come from our ability to genuinely feel and express gratitude and to be of service to others.

Whenever I notice myself having a pity party or complaining about some small, insignificant problem, I realize that the best way out of that kind of self-centered thinking is to get busy counting my blessings and looking for ways to help someone else. Always, without fail, being grateful and helping others immediately changes my energy and brings a smile to my face and heart. There are millions of ways to be of service just waiting for you to notice them.

Experiencing true gratitude in our hearts and minds has a positive and even healing effect on us. We feel happier when we see and acknowledge the blessings in our lives.

When life lessons are learned, insights and realizations come into our awareness. More and more, we notice the gifts, blessings, and miracles that surround us every day. We appreciate what we have and who we are because we understand how precious life is and how important relationships are.

Appreciate and bless the food you eat, the home that shelters you, the car that transports you and gives you the freedom to travel. Bless your finances and your ability to pay your bills. Bless your body and be grateful for all that it allows you to do. Be grateful for all of the blessings and lessons in your life. Your conscious awareness of the daily good in your life will keep you in a state of appreciation.

This ability to recognize, to really see, and to be thankful for beauty and blessings gives us an expanded sense of the sacred and divine. Feeling grateful is a gourmet meal of soul food that nourishes our body, mind, and spirit, giving us the motivation and power to be more and to give more.

As we are filled with gratitude and appreciation, we are able to give to others from the overflow. This is true service: the ability to give from the abundance of love, peace, and happiness within us which spills out onto others as joyful service and is always for the greatest good of all.

Make sure that you include a heartfelt practice of being grateful for all of the beauty, blessings, gifts, miracles (big and small), opportunities to learn and grow, insights, aha moments, and whatever else you can find to appreciate. As you do this, more and more, you will be inspired to serve in ways you never could have imagined. And that service will be an unbelievable source of motivation and power to you and others.

I cannot emphasize how much light is added to our world and how much darkness is dispelled by kindness, gratitude, and service. These are incredible MAPS because they keep you in the present moment and are motivation and power sources for you, the giver, and for the person receiving your gifts of kindness and service.

Gratitude is probably the most potent of MAPS. When we truly feel grateful and thankful, content in heart and mind, we are our best selves, radiating positive energy wherever we are.

Here are five easy gratitude MAPS for daily use:

- Upon waking, think of things you are thankful for.
- Throughout the day, think about your blessings.
- Throughout the day, look for the good and appreciate it.
- Throughout the day, smile and say thank you often.
- Go to bed with a smile on your face and gratitude in your heart.

♥   ♥   ♥

"Give thanks for the morning light. Give thanks for your life and strength. Give thanks for your food. Give thanks for your abilities and talents. And if you see no reason to give thanks, rest assured, the fault is yours."

—Paraphrased from anonymous Native American wisdom
(Sometimes attributed to Chief Tecumseh)

♥   ♥   ♥

"I slept and dreamt that life was joy. I awoke and saw that life was service. I acted and behold, service was joy."

—Rabindranath Tagore

∽♡ Create to Integrate ♡∽

Take a few minutes to sit quietly and think about some things for which you are grateful. Think about anyone and anything you appreciate and are thankful for. List at least seven here.

_____

_____

_____

_____

_____

_____

Now take a few more minutes to think about things you can do, actions you can take, to be of service to someone. Who are some people you can help, and what are some causes you believe in and would like to contribute, volunteer time, energy, or resources to? List at least seven here.

_____

_____

_____

_____

_____

_____

If you want or need additional space to list more, just keep going on this page and refer to it often as a reminder of how blessed you are.

You can add to and refer to these lists any time you want to feel better. Gratitude and service will always uplift you and change your thoughts and feelings.

Chapter 11

Action and Activity MAPS

Any action or activity that causes you to feel better than you did prior to doing it is a source of motivation and power. If they bring you into the present moment and keep you there, they can easily be considered MAPS.

Every morning, before getting out of bed, I say a prayer, then go for a walk, do energization exercises, and meditate. This is my way of starting the day. These few, simple actions make a big difference in the way I think and feel. My intention is to bring calm, kindness, and compassion into each day, and these actions help me do that.

Actions that lead you to or put you in a state of gratitude, appreciation, and reverence are MAPS as well. Activities like meditation, prayer, breathing exercises, Reiki, Ho'oponopono, may seem like somewhat passive activities, but they can profoundly change you. Movements and exercises like yoga, t'ai chi ch'uan, and qi gong positively affect your body, mind, and spirit, so they can be sources of motivation and power for you too.

Volunteering your time and energy to causes that you believe in and want to support, as well as being of service and helping others, always leaves us feeling better; we receive so much more than we give.

Lending a helping hand to a family member, friend, or stranger, responding to an unexpected need, and being a part-time companion to a senior or a child are just a few examples of actions that are MAPS. They are sources of motivation and power to both the giver and the receiver. Even a sincere smile is an action taken that can make a difference.

The words we use and the actions we choose do make a difference. Are we contributing to the positive or adding to the negative? This world and all of us here need more positive words and actions. Be MAPS to yourself and others through the choices you make, the words you speak, and the actions you take.

The following are just a few more activities that can bring us into the present moment and be MAPS for us: kayaking, singing, gardening, snorkeling, playing a musical instrument, hiking, reviewing this guidebook, dancing, painting, and walking your dog. You can probably think of hundreds more. Just do the activities that you enjoy and they will be sources of motivation and power for you.

Whenever that old committee meets and your thinking spirals downward, do something to bring yourself into the present moment and redirect your thoughts and energy in a positive direction.

An example might be something like this: A personal pity party takes over your brain and you find yourself feeling victimized ("poor me"), complaining and blaming. Get up, go watch some funny or inspirational videos on YouTube, make a delicious meal and take it to a homeless person, make some MAPS—do anything that will motivate and empower you to think and feel better.

Smile and laugh often. It can actually change your brain chemistry immediately. It's not possible to think sad thoughts with a genuine, heartfelt smile on your face. And laughter is the best medicine. If you can't muster up a smile, just go to the mirror and push the sides of your lips up with your hands. If that process doesn't make you smile, you'll laugh at the funny grin looking back at you.

Whatever actions and activities motivate and empower you are your MAPS. Something that works for you may not work for someone else. And you may find that something that motivated you in the past no longer has the same power for you now. Do what you love and what you enjoy doing. If you love cooking, swimming, or sculpting, do that. If it motivates and empowers you, if it keeps you in the present moment, then it's one of your MAPS.

Just keep identifying the actions and activities that keep you in the present moment, the conscious now. Do what helps you think and feel better so you're the best you can be.

"All truly successful action comes out of that field of alert attention, rather than from ego and conditioned, unconscious thinking."

—Eckhart Tolle, *A New Earth*

❧ Create to Integrate ❧

Make a list of seven activities that you enjoy and that bring you into the present, uplift you, motivate you, and empower you to think, feel, and be your best.

_____

_____

_____

_____

_____

_____

_____

How do the above actions affect your state of mind and how you feel?

_____

_____

_____

_____

_____

_____

_____

Which actions/activities are the three best MAPS (motivation and power sources) for you and why?

1. _____

_____

2. _____

_____

3. _____

_____

Keep adding to this list, refer to it, and do these actions/activities.

Chapter 12

Meditation and Breathing MAPS

As mentioned in the previous chapter, some activities are more passive in nature, yet still they are actions that can be awesome sources of motivation, inspiration, and empowerment.

We all have experienced the benefit of taking several deep, slow breaths to calm a feeling of fear, anxiety, or anger. Those deep, slow breaths bring us into the present and give us pause to reevaluate what's going on. Conscious breathing is accessible to all of us all the time, and it works.

Meditation, prayer, chanting, the use of mantras and affirmations, Ho'oponopono, breath and pranayama techniques like Hong Sau, Kriya, and yogic breathing are, undeniably, MAPS. They bring us into present-moment *now* consciousness and into a clearer uplifted state than we were in prior to doing them because they calm the restless mind.

These activities absolutely change the way we think and feel. We are given calm and clarity that leads us to make better choices and decisions. The scientific community recognizes the power and benefit of meditation and controlled-breathing exercises.

Investigate and explore the many activities in this passive category to find the ones that are MAPS for you. Though they are calming in nature, they will have a profound influence on you as you do them more and more frequently. The cumulative effect increases each time you do them, and you will find yourself thinking and feeling better and better.

Review Chapter 9 to see how important it is to create daily rituals, routines, and practices that can keep you centered and calm so you can go out and be in the world in the most positive and productive way possible. It is so helpful for us to feel strengthened and empowered to be and contribute our best each day.

For many years, I have used meditation and breathing for centering and calming myself, always with positive results and a cumulative influence of inner power and peace.

Our lives are filled with challenges large and small. The more MAPS we have and use, the more likely it is that we will find the peace of heart and mind that our bodies and souls crave. It takes conscious, consistent determination and action to rise above the difficulties, but your MAPS will be the way.

The school of life asks us each day, "How did you show up?", "What did you learn?", and "What did you give back in gratitude for the awakening of this life of opportunity?" Your meditation and breathing MAPS are important allies for living the answers to these questions and just feeling good.

♥   ♥   ♥

"You may be surprised at what seclusion with God will do for your mind, body and soul....Through the portals of silence, the healing sun of wisdom and peace will shine upon you."

—Paramahansa Yogananda, *Man's Eternal Quest*

♥   ♥   ♥

"The biological wonder of a breath is so easy to take for granted, but every now and again I get still enough to notice it. And when I do: Wow! I stand in awe of the miracle that life is."

—Oprah Winfrey, *O Magazine*

Chapter 13

Intention and Willpower

As you learn, grow, shift, and change throughout life, some of your MAPS will too. The intensity and meaning of something that motivated and empowered you at a certain time in your life may change, but as long as it brings you into the present moment, it is still serving you as a source of motivation and power.

What's important is that you continue accessing new and even more powerful MAPS for yourself.

In reading this guidebook, I hope you have come to realize that motivation and power sources are everywhere and that they vary from person to person. What may be MAPS for one person don't necessarily serve as MAPS for another.

Music, art, poetry, people, and places—everything has different value and meaning to each of us. The astounding beauty and variation of roses are great MAPS for me, yet to someone else, they may be merely pretty flowers. A piece of music that is a source of motivation and power for you may just be good listening to me, but not inspiring. We are all motivated by different things. What pulls one person into the present moment may go completely unnoticed by someone else.

Be concerned only with what supports your growth, well-being, peace of heart and mind, and what helps you to feel the best you can feel and be the best you can be. When you are focused on what you need to do to change your mind chatter, moods, and actions, you become a better influence on others.

One of the main purposes of MAPS is to give you the wherewithal to set clear intentions for yourself and your life and to invoke the willpower necessary for you to manifest your intentions.

What are intention and willpower? Intention is a purpose, aim, or goal. Will is the power of conscious, deliberate action or choice; willing something is the act or experience of exercising this power with strong determination and self-control.

Your motivation and power sources bring you into the present moment, where clear intentions can be set and where your willpower will be ignited and fueled. Your MAPS are your own personal inspiration to keep your willpower strong and to keep yourself actively pursuing your goals (intentions). Use your MAPS to the present moment to help you stick to it until you succeed.

Visualize with feeling your intention manifested, and use your detailed, focused attention, your creative abilities, and your patience to enhance the willpower necessary to accomplish your goal. Paramahansa Yogananda says that no matter how impossible the accomplishment of a goal may seem, you must never stop repeating conscious acts of determination and will to achieve it. He says, "A strong will, by its own dynamic force, creates a way for fulfillment of its intention."

Research has shown us that the brain has neuroplasticity; this means that we can install new ways of thinking into our brains, just like a computer can be given new input and reprogrammed to work in new ways. Retrain your brain to work for you, not against you. Use this knowledge to think and act in productive, not destructive ways.

The way we think can be changed by new data (information) and by learning to create cohesion with our thoughts and feelings so they are aligned to magnetize desired outcomes. According to quantum physics, everything is energy; this is what all the true wisdom teachings have told us all along.

For example, consider the following: You wake up on the wrong side of the bed, feeling grumpy and thinking, "Oh no, it's going to be a yucky day." You pull yourself out of bed and open the curtains to find that it's cloudy outside (just like your brain this morning). You go to make coffee and realize you're out of coffee filters, so you figure you'll leave early to stop by Starbucks. By now you're even grumpier, and the committee chimes in. "No sunshine, no coffee—I'm going to be late. What next? Blah, blah, blah..."

You can see that this day is now off to a rough start, and if it keeps going in this direction, the chances of its being a happy, peaceful one are not good. The worse you feel, the worse you think, and the worse you think, the worse you feel.

Let's go the other way. You wake up and, before rolling out of bed, take a good stretch and a deep breath or two. Then you affirm to yourself or out loud, "Good morning! Let this day begin." Open the curtains to the cloudy sky and notice how interesting the clouds are in color and shape. Purposefully say thank you for this new day. Go into it with gratitude and wonder, or at least with optimistic curiosity because the better you think, the better you feel, and the better you feel, the better you think.

Set your intentions daily and use all the MAPS necessary to invoke, strengthen, and sustain your willpower. Take conscious actions toward your intended goals. Each day, remind yourself to create a new mind. Old beliefs, fears, habits, and ways of thinking and feeling that no longer serve you will change into new possibilities.

Every day, all the time, we are generating energy. Negative or positive energy is going out of us into the world to either decrease or increase its vibrational frequency based on what we are thinking and feeling. Are we emitting low-frequency energy, like sadness, anger, or fear, or high-frequency vibrations like joy, compassion, and love?

As we improve ourselves, we become better friends because our example and influence helps everyone around us. Use your MAPS to be a high-vibrational-frequency generator, to think and feel your best, and to live the best version of yourself.

♥   ♥   ♥

"Be the change you wish to see in the world."

—Mahatma Gandhi

♥ Create to Integrate ♥

Sit quietly for a few minutes and think about some daily intentions you would like to set for yourself. Get as clear, detailed, and specific as possible. For example, instead of writing something like "I will exercise more," write "I will walk twenty minutes every other day. When weather permits, I will walk outside, and if the weather prohibits my walking outside, I will walk on a treadmill inside or at the local indoor mall. I won't be deterred." Visualize yourself walking, how you will feel walking, and where you will walk.

List at least three daily intentions:

1. _____

_____

2. _____

_____

3. _____

_____

Which MAPS will help you focus and strengthen your will to follow through on the above intentions? (For example: listening to music or an inspirational CD, repeating a positive affirmation or statement of gratitude while walking.)

Lists some MAPS that will invoke and sustain your willpower to accomplish the above intentions. List MAPS that will keep you in the present and overcome any unwanted negative chatter from the committee.

1. _____

_____

2. _____

_____

3. _____

_____

Chapter 14

Making MAPS to the Present Moment

When you're making MAPS, there is no need for artistic talent; it's a fun right- and left-brain activity. This is a place where your creativity can play and express itself.

However, every word and image you use *must* be something that inspires you and gives you a positive feeling.

Here are some possible motivation and power sources:

- power words
- power phrases
- inspirational sayings, quotes
- photos of people, places, or things
- gratitude pages (things that you are grateful for)
- poetry
- books
- music
- inspiring and uplifting movies
- motivational tapes or CDs
- guided visualizations
- bright ideas, insights, inspirations, or realizations
- daydreams, imaginings, wishes, desires
- affirmations

- paintings, drawings, sketches that you create
- other art
- stickers (happy faces, butterflies, stars, angels, etc.)
- talismans and sacred objects
- divination cards
- any of the Create to Integrate pages from this guidebook or any new ones you create
- any other idea, object, or article that inspires you

Remember, for something to be a motivation and power source, it must

- be something that motivates you in a positive way;
- be a power source to you;
- inspire you;
- move you to change your thoughts, moods, and actions;
- be defined as powerful, inspirational, and motivational; and
- bring you into present-moment consciousness.

Materials needed for making MAPS:

- scissors
- glue or paste
- clear scotch tape
- pens, pencils, markers, paint, crayons
- magazines and books that you can cut or copy

Use your imagination. Anything that inspires you is what you need.

As you know by now, some of your MAPS should be things that you carry with you and have around you, anywhere you are, at any time. I suggest that you use any of the following to make your MAPS portable and accessible.

- a book with different sections, some lined pages for writing, some blank pages for pasting or drawing, pockets for special mementos, and plastic photo holders
- 3x5 or 5x7 index cards, card stock, greeting cards, etc.
- a photo album

- envelopes
- a small purse, bag, or pouch
- a small box or container
- a plastic business-card holder

Use your imagination to find what works for you.

Start by getting quiet and receptive to your inner guidance leading the way. Find, gather, and create as many things from the above list of possible motivation and power sources. Put them into your book, box, container, pouch, or envelope. Put your MAPS on walls, mirrors, tables, anywhere you will see them frequently.

I have several books of various sizes containing MAPS that I have gathered and created for myself, and I also carry pouches containing sacred objects and cards with motivational sayings and affirmations written on them. This way, I have them with me at all times; you never know when you will need them. I have MAPS all around my home and on my smartphone. In my car, I make sure to have CDs of music and motivational speakers that uplift and inspire me.

When you are just beginning to use your MAPS, I suggest that you refer to them often, at least once in the morning and once at night. This will allow you to see and feel how they are working for you.

Be sure that you have them with you at all times so that you can use them to redirect your thinking, guide you to a better feeling, and remind you of who you really are and where you want to be in body, mind, and spirit.

Soon you will find that just touching or thinking about your MAPS works as well as if you were creating them or looking at them. I always enjoy going through my MAPS and I find myself getting more and more motivation and power from them each time. I add to them and change them occasionally, as needed.

Remember, there is no right or wrong way to do this. However, it is imperative that no negative words or images are used. Avoid anything that is counter to your focus. Find what inspires you. Your sources will be different from anyone else's. Each one is an individual, creative expression.

MAPS are motivation and power sources that bring you into the present moment, where your negative thinking can be changed into positive thinking, where bad feelings can be changed into better ones, and where you are uplifted and inspired to take positive action.

A word, group of words, phrase, poem, or quote can stimulate your imagination and motivate and empower you.

Beach Days Ocean Breezes

Blissful Moments HEALING

the power of nature

A picture, photo, drawing, or painting can be a visual stimulation that motivates and empowers you.

An experience itself can be a source of motivation and power.

GO TO THE OCEAN

Listening to a recording of rhythmic ocean waves or music that incorporates this sound can be an auditory stimulation that motivates and empowers you.

All of these are MAPS if they motivate, empower, uplift, and inspire you and bring you into the present moment.

∽♡ Create to Integrate ♡∽

Now make some MAPS that you can carry with you in your purse or pocket or put on a wall at home, in your office or workspace, or in your car.

Get your materials together and sit quietly, allowing your inner guidance to lead you. Use your creativity and imagination and remember that there is no right or wrong way to do this.

This is a process to keep you in the present in a positive way. The MAPS you make will uplift, motivate, inspire, and empower you when you refer to them later.

Enjoy and have fun.

Chapter 15

MAPS for Family and Friends

Everyone likes to receive something unexpected, and when it's something that has been made especially for them, it is very special.

It's really fun to make MAPS for family members and friends. As it turns out, these MAPS are a gift for them and for you, as well. You will feel good making them and giving them. All of the MAPS that I have made and given have been received with enthusiasm and appreciation.

The recipients have said that the MAPS make them feel good and are a source of unexpected inspiration and motivation. Often, people have told me that they came at just the right time, when they needed some encouragement or support. Others have said that they look at the MAPS often and feel uplifted when they do so.

When making MAPS for others, I hold that person in my heart and mind. As I am thinking about them, I receive ideas, words, and pictures that I feel will uplift and inspire them. The process seems to become a kind of meditation, and I find myself being guided to just the right words and images for that person.

This is an exercise in being in the present moment in a creative way. This creative energy makes me feel good and helps me feel even more inspired. Making MAPS for family members and friends is a motivation and power source for me too.

When you make MAPS for others, you are giving them a gift of inspiration. You are acknowledging their value and giving them encouragement and support. You are showing them how you see them, how you feel about them, and that you believe in them and care about them. Everyone wants to feel that they are important to someone and that they are thought of in loving ways. The MAPS you make for them do exactly that.

You can refer to the previous chapter for suggested materials and ideas. I often enhance birthday cards, thank-you cards, and blank cards with words, pictures, and quotes that I think a person will find uplifting, inspiring, or amusing.

This doesn't require artistic talent; just use your own imagination and creativity and enjoy the process. I guarantee that the recipient of your thoughtful MAPS will enjoy them too.

Create to Integrate

Make some MAPS for a family member or friend. Remember that there is no right or wrong way to make MAPS. Just use your creativity and imagination and let your inner guidance lead the way.

When you give these MAPS to the people you have made them for, you'll be surprised at how much they enjoy them and use them as a source of joy and inspiration. The MAPS will definitely put smiles on their faces and in their hearts.

Chapter 16

Circle of Love MAPS

The Circle of Love is another format for MAPS (motivation and power sources). They are for both the person *making* the circle and the person who is *in* the circle. I first discovered a similar technique over thirty-five years ago from a sweet friend, Dorothy Clark, who was, at the time, in her late eighties. She told me it was a way of sending healing energy and love to someone in need, or just an energetic protection for someone you love and care about. I did it for my family and friends.

It was not until I began writing this guidebook that I was reminded of this powerful tool. The angels showed me that it is indeed another format MAPS can take because it is a source of motivation and power for both the person in the circle and the person who puts them there.

My guidance has also expanded my understanding and revealed deeper meaning. The circle is actually a sphere that is around each of us at all times. Holographic in nature, it is like an answered prayer that one is already grateful for.

Like making MAPS for yourself or family or friends, making Circle of Love MAPS is another exercise which brings you into the present moment in a creative way and is a source of motivation and power.

When I make a Circle of Love, I visualize the person in the center of the sphere surrounded by their angels, guides, helpers, healers, masters, and teachers. I see love and light coming to them from the Infinite Source of All That Is.

I then put a picture of the person or just their name in the center of the circle and find myself attracting just the right words, phrases, quotes, or pictures that will be inspiring and empowering to them. Placing these words, etc. inside and outside of the circle makes this a visual as well as an energetic tool for them and for me. I see them receiving the healing, insights, realizations, strength, and courage to overcome any obstacle, and I see them trusting that Infinite Source is at work at all times. I trust that the person is protected and all is well.

The Circle of Love helps me immensely whenever I worry about my children or other loved ones. It shifts my thinking from helpless worrying to empowered visualization. I am holding a greater, more positive, and powerful truth for them and for myself, and they are benefiting energetically as well.

I often send them a copy of the Circle of Love that I have made, and they are grateful to know that I see them as healthy, happy, safe, capable, and strong. This Circle of Love then becomes a motivation and power source for them.

I always carry with me a Circle of Love with my three sons in the center. I have given them Circle of Love MAPS so they can see that I believe they have all of the resources necessary to overcome any obstacle and be the best they can be, and that everything is in place for them to succeed.

I have a larger Circle of Love that I use at home whenever anyone (including me) is in special need of support, encouragement, protection, or healing. There is a heart shape in the center of the circle, and I place a picture of them or their name inside the heart. (See the template at the end of the chapter). Sometimes I am guided to pull divination cards and put them around the circle as added insight and information. When I look at this circle, I hold a vision of the person receiving the love, support, and protection, and I see them feeling better as a result of the positive healing energy that is surrounding them. Instead of feeling and sending worry, fear, or doubt, I feel and send positive, loving energy, and I trust that Infinite Source is operating at all times and that whatever is needed for their support and success is available and accessible. A feeling of gratitude always engulfs me in this process.

Make Circle of Love MAPS for yourself too so that you can be reminded whenever it's necessary that everything is in divine order; all is well. You are always surrounded with love and light, and Infinite Source is providing you with all that you need to learn, grow, and succeed in life with peace of heart and mind.

"Come out of the circle of time and into the circle of love."

—Rumi

"The whole earth, the solar system, the far-flung galaxies and island universes—everything is floating in this vast sphere of love. Feel, meditate on, merge yourself in that love which permeates and upholds the infinitude of manifestation—a demonstrable presence of God's heartbeat of bliss."

—Paramahansa Yogananda, *The Second Coming of Christ*

Template of a Circle of Love

This is a sample template of a Circle of Love for you to use or to adapt to your liking.

❤ Create to Integrate ❤

Create a Circle of Love for a family member, friend, or yourself. Remember that there is no right or wrong way to make MAPS. Use your creativity and let your inner guidance lead the way.

Sit quietly for a few moments and think about the person you are creating the Circle of Love for. You will be guided to the words, pictures, affirmations, or quotes to use.

Put a picture or write the name of the person inside of the heart in the center of the circle. Write, paste, glue the words, quotes, etc. around them in and outside of the circle as if they are surrounded by all of the loving energy you have placed there for them. You are holding a vision of them healthy, happy and successful.

Most importantly, just enjoy the process, be creative, and have fun for that is the positive energy that you want to send.

Chapter 17

Soul Food

Are you appeasing your senses or pleasing your soul? Our self-centered minds are always concerned with getting pleasure and avoiding pain. Our senses are fed by the ego's demands—"I want this," "I don't like that"—of immediate gratification to satisfy every whim, sensation, or feeling. It is always looking for ways to quench a thirst or feed a hunger. And yet, the thirst and the hunger are the soul's longing for a soothing, deep connection with life and Spirit.

Are you feeding yourself unsatisfying tidbits, or are you going for real soul food? Soul food is what brings deep, lasting peace, contentment, and joy. Tidbits are like a drive-through fast food, in contrast to lovely meals made with love and care, with each bite to be savored and enjoyed. Soul food is the relaxing bath with music and candles, as opposed to a quick shower taken in a rush to get somewhere else.

We all know what it's like to satisfy sensual pleasures, only to end up realizing that the solution is only partially or temporarily satisfying, if not completely unsatisfying.

Our senses, emotions, and feelings want satisfaction at any cost, while the soul is willing to take a little time and move at a slower pace. The ego languishes over opportunities it missed or might miss, while the soul knows that every moment is a new opportunity.

When we're not in the present moment, we are reaching into the past or the future, listening to the stories and judgments of that old committee. Here are some distinctions between appeasing the senses and pleasing the soul:

- An uncomfortable feeling comes up, and to appease the senses, we eat something, watch TV, or sleep—we do anything to cover it up, avoid it, or make it go away.
- An uncomfortable feeling comes up and, to please the soul, you take a walk in nature and feast your eyes on the surrounding beauty, as you open your heart and mind to the blessings, or sit under a beautiful, old tree in receptive silence. Inhale, exhale, just breathe. Slow down your pace and look for the good.

Our souls are also being fed when time disappears

- in deep meditation;
- in meaningful conversation with a friend or colleague;
- in the flow of a really good jam session;
- during a creative project or endeavor;
- at a great movie, in an compelling book, or in beautiful music; and
- while doing anything else that keeps us in the present moment and fully engaged.

When we go for pleasing the soul, we end up pleasing the senses as well. Remember, your MAPS will always help you because they are

- keeping you in the present moment;
- something that you love and enjoy;
- diminishing negative self-talk, judgment, and criticism; and
- motivating and empowering you to make good choices and take positive action.

You might not be able to make big changes all at once, but small, steady steps will feed your soul and lead you to feeling more satisfied. Here are some MAPS that might work for you:

- Take a short walk in the fresh air instead of having another cup of coffee.
- Slowly savor and enjoy the first and last bites of a meal if you're not ready to slow down for the entire thing.
- Go to a yoga class.
- Enjoy a massage or a pedicure.
- Be with people who motivate you and go to places that inspire you.
- Volunteer for causes and projects you believe in.
- Do things you love and enjoy more often; smile, laugh, sing, and dance.

The possibilities are endless. Use the MAPS that work best for you because they will inspire you to give yourself the soul food of life that deeply nurtures and empowers you to be the best you can be.

Chapter 18

Your MAPS: A Thrive-All Kit

Many say that we need a survival kit to be prepared for a big disaster such as an earthquake, a hurricane, a terrorist attack, or any other serious emergency.

I think we need a "thrive-all" kit. Something to help us not only survive, but also thrive in any and all conditions and circumstances. Not just for the big challenges, but also for the everyday challenges we face on an ongoing basis.

Staying confident in these constantly changing times and maintaining our self-esteem through job loss, criticism, or rejection is challenging. It is a constant vigil to turn negative or limiting thoughts and feelings into more positive ones and to overcome the self-talk that debilitates and discourages us. It requires continual determination to stay focused and on course to our dreams and desires and to turn our so-called failures into successes, our doubt into optimism, our confusion into clarity.

The MAPS to the present moment that you have identified, discovered, and created are the very things that make up your personal thrive-all kit. Here is everything you need to stay motivated and empowered to make changes in yourself, to stay strong and inspired to take positive action, and to feel and be the best that you can be.

Whenever a challenge, disaster, crisis, or upset comes, you have what you need to thrive in any condition, circumstance, or situation. You have what you need to maintain a positive attitude and be empowered to move through any difficulty in the most positive way.

We all want more than just to survive something; we want to be able to thrive in any and all conditions. I don't consider myself a cancer survivor, but a thriver. To survive means to live or exist beyond death or an occurrence, while to thrive means to be successful, to grow with vigor, to flourish. The more you know, the more you grow. The more you are prepared, the better you can handle anything that happens and the better you become from each experience.

I remember the day the doctor told me I had breast cancer. He said, "The most important thing you *must* do is get a team together. More than anything, a team is what you will need to get through this." He was right. I put together a team of family and friends whom I knew would be there for me and not let me wallow in fear, who would hold a vision of me healthy and strong. These dear ones would motivate and empower me to move forward. They were and still are incredible MAPS when I really need them. I spent time in places that were points of power for me, and I put myself in positive, uplifting situations. I surrounded myself with inspiring books, music, and people.

I made many, many new MAPS and I constantly referred to the ones I already had. I connected with anything and everything that motivated and empowered me, recognized the many blessings in my life every day, and found myself supporting and encouraging others as I recovered. I created a thrive-all kit that continues to grow and expand. These MAPS always help me find my way to a better place inside me.

Your thrive-all kit should contain everything that is a motivation and power source for you. Carry these MAPS with you; have them around you at home, on your smartphone, in your workplace, on your computer, in your car— wherever they can be available to help you when you need them. Use them to think your best thoughts, to feel your best, to make the best choices and decisions, to set clear intentions, and to fuel your willpower to take the best action and have the best life you can.

Along everyone's road in life, there are peaks and valleys, highways and potholes, smooth sailing and construction zones. Use your MAPS as your own personal GPS to help navigate the terrain. Let your motivation and power sources make traveling easier and guide your way. Enjoy the journey.

We all have challenges; we all get distracted and pulled out of the present. Sometimes we unconsciously eat more than is necessary for our health or well-being, or watch too much television, or get stuck on the cell phone or the computer, or drift into past or future thinking, or get caught up in current problems, dramas, etc.

So much pulls us out of the conscious *now*. It takes a lot to stay focused and positive. My prayer is that what is offered in this guidebook will help you in some way and each day to find your way to the peace and presence of love in you and all around you.

Boundless blessings.

Chapter 19

MAPS Gatherings and Support Groups

MAPS to the present moment are your way through tough times and emotions. They can help you thrive in any situation or circumstance. The material in this guidebook has given you tools, insights, and ideas to enhance your ability to change negative and limiting thinking to positive possibility thinking. You have learned how to identify and create motivation and power sources for yourself and to change your definitions and perceptions to feel better about whatever you are experiencing.

Share this material with friends. Get together with others who are interested in thinking, feeling, and being more positive. Remember, "The company you keep is stronger than your will," and "Where two or more are gathered, the energy is magnified."

Create a support group of like-minded people and meet at least once a month (or more often if possible) to make MAPS together, exchange ideas, and share MAPS that work for you and could inspire and uplift others. Use this as a time to share positive solutions and talk about possibilities.

These are times to come together more, not to withdraw and separate yourself. Be there to encourage one another, but don't use these gatherings for complaining or blaming. Let your MAPS support groups be about truly supporting each other in positive ways. If you've read an inspiring book, seen an uplifting movie, or heard a new song that made you feel happy, share it. Share anything that is a motivation and power source to you and that could possibly be a motivation and power source to someone else.

You'll find that these gatherings will themselves be MAPS too because they will be stimulating, uplifting, and fun.

Everyone has something to offer. What people love and enjoy are great MAPS to share. I love getting together with friends who share their interests and passions. One friend facilitates a group called A Course in Miracles, which she loves, and another friend is an event producer who is always turning me on to beautiful things and ideas. Yet another friend is deeply into crystals and sound healing while some other friends often share information on the healing powers of flowers and essential oils—all kinds of fun and interesting things.

Get together and share what you love and enjoy. From cooking to reiki, quilting to gardening, hiking to horseback riding, share your favorites with friends. You'll find that these times together are MAPS, keeping you in the present moment together. You might learn something new and you will certainly enjoy each other's company. You see, motivation and power sources are everywhere; everyone has some to share.

Enjoy.

Chapter 20

Introduction to Parent-Child and Teacher-Student Activities

For thirty-five-plus years, I worked extensively with children from preschool through high school. I've spent years in classrooms and designed and implemented numerous projects and programs for young people and adults.

The one thing that I found common and prevalent across all age groups is the need for activities that empower and support confidence and self-esteem. Consequently, all of my work has an underlying foundation that builds and strengthens each person's ability to believe in himself or herself.

Building, strengthening, supporting, and empowering one's self-esteem and confidence is an ongoing, lifelong process of gathering tools and resources and learning what motivates and inspires us.

To boost our self-esteem and feel confident, we must utilize any and all activities, people, and resources available to us. When we do so, we can feel motivated and empowered to go for our goals, and we have a greater sense of our ability to succeed.

We all want this for ourselves and for our children. The more tools we can give our youth to help them feel more confident, the better equipped they will be to make better choices and decisions for themselves. The more techniques they have to change negative thinking into positive thoughts and actions, the more likely they will use them to feel better and make better choices for themselves.

The following MAPS activities are for parents to do with their children and for teachers to do with their students. These activities are a template for helping youth start identifying, finding, making, and using motivation and power sources for themselves.

Parents and teachers know their children and students better than anyone else does. You are in an expert position to help them. It is not necessary to follow the activity exactly as it is written; use your intuition to make the activity as productive, fun, and beneficial as it can be.

Most of all, enjoy your time together and the process. Much will be revealed and you will be given opportunities to see and learn what your children and students need and how you can help them feel more confident and able to succeed.

These activities are openings into deeper connections in which you can discover how youth can be motivated to make positive choices and take inspired, positive actions. When you are engaged in positive activities with your children, they are not only receiving positive messages, but also are being influenced by your example. Play, have fun, and be creative to support and strengthen their confidence and self-esteem.

Use these activities as a beginning and as a template to create even more MAPS activities with your children and students and to encourage them to come up with more ideas.

Enjoy.

Chapter 21

Activities for Parents and Children

Parent–Child Activity A: Create to Integrate

1. Tell your child that today you are going to do an activity that will be fun and something they can do any time in order to feel good. The activity is called MAPS to the Present Moment.

2. Ask your child what a map is and what it's used for. Let them give you their definitions. Be sure their answers include the following points:
   - Maps show people how to get from one place to another.
   - When we're lost or confused, a map shows us the way to get to where we want to go.

3. Explain to your child that today they will think about and talk about people, places, situations, and things that will help them change unhappy thoughts and feelings to happy ones.

4. Give them the following example (or another one that is appropriate for your child): Let's say you're feeling sad and you want to feel better. MAPS will help you change your thoughts and feelings because they give you the motivation and power to change.

5. Ask your child what *motivation* and *power* mean. Be sure they understand that motivation makes us feel like doing something and

power is like the energy that makes us do it. (Refer to Chapter 1, What Are MAPS to the Present Moment?)

6. Explain that MAPS (motivation and power sources) are anyone or anything that helps us feel better and more confident to make good choices and decisions.

7. Go over Chapter 6, Who, Where, What MAPS. Read it to your child or paraphrase it according to their age and understanding. Be sure they understand before continuing.

8. Give them the first Create to Integrate page about people, places, situations, and things. (If necessary, modify it to suit your child.) Go over the directions with them and have them complete the first section about people. Discuss their answers and ask questions to be sure they understand that the people they have chosen are ones with whom they feel happy.

9. Have them do the next section about places and, as you did with the previous section, talk about these places that are special to them and make them feel good.

10. Now do the section on situations and talk with them about how these situations make them feel good.

11. Have them do the section on things and discuss their choices as you have in the previous sections.

12. Allowing sufficient time for the activity, help them find a place where they can keep their MAPS so they can refer to them and feel good whenever they want to. Remind them that all of the people, places, situations, and things which they listed in today's activity are MAPS (motivation and power sources).

13. When you have completed the activity, as you clean up together, ask them what they thought of this activity and how it made them feel.

14. Conclude by telling your child that MAPS help us feel good. "Whenever feelings are not so good, go to your MAPS to feel better. Anyone or anything that helps you think and feel better is a source of motivation and power; those are MAPS for you. You can add more to the lists at any time."
    - For similar MAPS activities go to #15.

15. If necessary, modify the other Create to Integrate pages in the guidebook to suit the age of your child. Read it to your child or paraphrase it, making sure they understand.
    - Go over the corresponding Create to Integrate page directions together and have them complete each one.
    - Discuss their answers and ask questions to be sure they understand.

Parent's note: This activity is designed to enhance self-esteem, boost confidence, and be an opportunity for you and your child to talk about feelings.

This curriculum outline is appropriate for children seven to eleven years old. For ages twelve and up, refer to the curriculum outline for Teacher–Student Activities.

Parent–Child Activity B: Making Maps

1. Ask your child again what a map is and what it's used for. Let them give you their definitions. Be sure their answers include the following points:
   - Maps show people how to get from one place to another.
   - When we're lost or confused, a map shows us the way to get to where we want to go.

2. Ask your child again what *motivation* and *power* mean. Be sure they understand that motivation makes us feel like doing something and power is like the energy that makes us do it.

3. Remind them that MAPS (motivation and power sources) help us feel better so we can make better choices and decisions.

4. Ask your child what they thought about the previous activity and what their favorite parts of it were.

5. Briefly go over their favorites from the previous activity and ask them how what they did made them feel. Ask the following questions:
   - Why are the people or places you listed sources of motivation and power to you, and how do they make you feel?
   - Why are certain situations and things MAPS (motivation and power sources) for you?

   Adjust the questions according to the Create to Integrate page you used.

6. Tell your child that today they will make some MAPS that will help them change "down" feelings to "up" feelings. These MAPS will help them to get from one feeling to another.

7. Give them the following example (or another one that is appropriate for your child): Let's say you're feeling sad and you want to feel better. Making MAPS or looking at ones you already have (like the pages from the previous activity) will help you to change your thoughts

and feelings because they will give you the motivation and power to change.

8. Explain again that MAPS (motivation and power sources) are anything that helps us feel better and more confident to make good choices and decisions.

9. Refer to Chapter 14, Making MAPS, and go over it with your child. Let them choose where they want to keep their MAPS: in a book, on 3x5 cards, in a box, taped to a wall in their room, etc.

10. Give your child a magazine and scissors and ask them to look through it and cut out anything they like that makes them feel good. Encourage them to cut out any words and pictures that inspire them.

11. After they have cut out some words and pictures, tell them that they can be as creative as they want to be.

12. Make sure they have glue, markers, paints, stickers, etc., and let them begin to make their own MAPS.

13. During the process of making MAPS, ask your child about the pictures, words, etc. that they are using and why those words and pictures make them feel good or are special to them.
   • Talk with them about how these words and pictures make them feel better, stronger, more confident, etc.
   • Encourage them with comments like, "You picked some powerful words for your MAPS". "I can see why that picture makes you feel good," and "Your creative ideas make me feel motivated to do this more."

14. Allowing sufficient time for the activity, help them find a place where they can keep their MAPS and MAPS-making materials so they can make more whenever they want to.

15. When you have completed the activity, as you clean up together, ask them what they thought of making MAPS and how it made them feel.

16. Conclude by telling your child that making MAPS makes us feel good. "Whenever your thoughts and feelings are not so good, go to your MAPS, or make more to think and feel better."

Parent's note: This activity is designed to enhance self-esteem, boost confidence, and be an opportunity for you and your child to talk about feelings.

This curriculum outline is appropriate for children seven to eleven years old. For ages twelve and up, refer to the curriculum outline for Teacher–Student Activities.

Chapter 22

Activities for Teachers and Students

Teacher—Student Activity A: Create to Integrate

1. Tell the students that today they are going to do an activity that will be fun and something they can do at any time to feel good. The activity is called MAPS to the Present Moment.

2. Ask the students what a map is and what it's used for. Let them give you their definitions. Be sure their answers include the following points:
   • Maps show people how to get from one place to another.
   • When we're lost or confused, maps show us the way to get to where we want to go.

3. Explain to your students that today's activity will help them change negative thoughts and feelings into positive ones. This activity will help them get from one feeling to another.

4. Give each student a copy of the poem "The Committee" and read it aloud or have a student do so. Ask them to give examples of the negative self-talk that goes on in our heads sometimes. Ask the students what they do to stop or change that negative self-talk.

5. Explain that MAPS (motivation and power sources) are a way of changing that negative thinking to positive thinking. They are self-help tools for thinking and feeling better. MAPS give us more confidence and can enhance our self-esteem.

6. Ask your students what *motivation* and *power* mean. Be sure they understand that motivation makes us feel like doing something and power is the fuel that makes us do it.

7. Refer to Chapter 1, What are MAPS to the Present Moment?, in this guidebook and explain that MAPS (motivation and power sources) are anything that helps us feel better and more confident so that we make good choices and decisions. (As an alternative, you can give each student a copy of Chapter 1 and read it aloud or have a student do so while the rest of the class follows along.)

8. Go over Chapter 6, Who, Where, What MAPS. Read it to the students or paraphrase it according to their age and understanding. Be sure they understand before continuing.

9. Give them the first Create to Integrate page about people, places, situations, and things. Go over the directions with them and have them complete the first section about people. Ask for volunteers to share who they chose and why those people are sources in motivation and power to them.

10. Have them do the next section about places and, as with the previous section, have volunteers talk about why the places they picked are special to them and make them feel good.

11. Now do the section on situations and have volunteers talk about how the situations they picked make them feel good and how they are sources of motivation and power.

12. Have them do the section on things and discuss their choices, as was done in the previous sections.

13. When you have completed the activity, ask the students what they thought about it and how it made them feel.

14. Explain that these lists are MAPS (sources of motivation and power). Urge them to keep MAPS with them, refer to them often, and find more things that can be used as MAPS.

15. Conclude by telling your students that MAPS help us think and feel better. "Whenever your thoughts or feelings are not so good, go to your MAPS to feel better. Think about, talk to and connect with the people on your list. Go to the places and create the situations that help you feel happy. Discover all the things that are motivation and power sources for you. Your MAPS will bring you into the present moment, where you can change negative self-talk and feel better about yourself."
    - For similar MAPS activities go to #16.

16. Use the other Create to Integrate pages in the guidebook. Read the chapter information to the students or paraphrase it, go over the directions together, and have students complete each one. Have them share their answers and ask questions to be sure they understand. Remind them each time that MAPS keep bringing us back to the conscious *now*, where we can change our negative self-talk and feel better about ourselves.

Teacher's note: This activity is designed to enhance self-esteem and boost confidence, and it is a self-help tool for changing negative thinking and feelings.

This curriculum outline is appropriate for children twelve and up. For ages seven to eleven, refer to the curriculum outline for Parent–Child Activities.

Teacher–Student Activity B: Making Maps

1. Ask your students again what a map is and what it's used for. Let them give you their definitions. Be sure their answers include the following points:
   - Maps show people how to get from one place to another.
   - When we're lost or confused, a map shows us the way to get to where we want to go.

2. Ask your students again what motivation and power mean. Be sure they understand that motivation makes us feel like doing something and power like the fuel that makes us do it.

3. Explain that MAPS (motivation and power sources) help us feel better so we can make better choices and decisions.

4. Ask your students what they thought about the previous activity and what their favorite parts of it were.

5. Briefly go over their favorites from the previous activity and ask them how what they did made them feel. Ask the following questions:
   - Why are the people or places you listed sources of motivation and power to you, and how do they make you feel?
   - Why are certain situations and things MAPS (motivation and power sources) for you?

   Adjust the questions according to the Create to Integrate page you used.

6. Tell your students that today, they will make some MAPS that will help them change negative thoughts and feelings to positive ones. These MAPS will help them to get from one feeling to another.

7. Give them the following example (or another one that is appropriate for your students): Let's say you're feeling sad and you want to feel better. Making MAPS or looking at ones you already have (like the pages from the previous activity) will help you to change your

thoughts and feelings because they will give you the motivation and power to change.

8. Explain again that MAPS (motivation and power sources) are anything that helps us feel better and more confident to make good choices and decisions.

9. Refer to Chapter 14, Making MAPS, and go over it with your students. Let them choose how they want to keep their MAPS: in a book, on 3x5 cards, in a box, taped to a wall in their room, etc. As this is a classroom activity, give each student a few 3x5 cards or a few pieces of construction paper or cardstock. If they have notebooks with blank pages, those can be used. Be creative.

10. Give each student a magazine and scissors and ask them to look through it and cut out anything they like that makes them feel good. Encourage them to cut out any words and pictures that are positive and inspiring.

11. After they have cut out some words and pictures, tell them that they can be as creative as they want to be.

12. Make sure they have glue, markers, paints, stickers, etc., and let them begin to make their own MAPS, putting their words and pictures on the 3x5 cards, paper, etc.

13. During the process of making MAPS, go around the room and ask your students about the pictures, and words that they are using and why those pictures and words make them feel good or are special to them.
    • Talk with the students about how these words and pictures make them feel better, stronger, and more confident.
    • Encourage them with comments like, "You picked some powerful words for your MAPS," "I can see why that picture makes you feel good," and "Your creative ideas make me feel motivated to do this more."

14. Allowing sufficient time for the activity, tell the students to think of a place to keep their MAPS (for example, a binder, a special book that they already have or can buy or create) where they will be accessible. (Give each student an envelope to put left-over words and/or pictures to use at another time.)

15. When you have completed the activity, as you clean up together, ask them what they thought of making MAPS and how it made them feel.

16. Conclude by telling the students that making MAPS makes us feel good. "When you're having a bad feeling, look at your MAPS, think about them, make more of them, and use them to bring you into the present moment, the conscious *now* where you can change negative thinking to positive thinking and feel better about yourself."

Teacher's note: This activity is designed to enhance self-esteem and boost confidence and it is a self-help tool for changing negative thinking and feelings.

This curriculum outline is appropriate for children twelve and up. For ages seven to eleven, refer to the curriculum outline for Parent–Child Activities.

Chapter 23

Conclusion

We are living in a time characterized by change. Circumstances change as fast as a channel surfer can flick a remote! What's in today is out tomorrow, and technology moves at a speed that makes what's at hand practically a dinosaur compared to what's coming out next week. Personal and global crises can take over in an instant, so we are constantly confronted with opportunities to rise or fall, to walk in fear or walk in faith.

So much that is happening calls us to conscious action—but sometimes all we want to do is roll over, pull the covers up over our heads, and go back to sleep!

But we can't sleep when our awareness has been awakened. And this is a time of awakening. It's a time when all resources must be called upon to help us find our way, strengthen our resolve, and commit to ourselves and one another to create a world that truly supports the good of all—a world where the best of who we are connects to support and celebrate life.

Time seems accelerated and nearly everyone is scrambling to make it through the day and make ends meet. Everything is moving quickly; we are finding it hard to make time for each other. Families and friends can rarely get together for a relaxing meal, let alone time to just talk, play, or even pray. *Life is precious and it can change in an instant.*

It's no wonder more and more people are taking bits of time to look within, ask important questions of themselves, and seek ways to find a deeper, more meaningful life. When it seems like there is no time, that is precisely when we must make time. And there is no time like the present!

We need anything and everything that can help us stay strong and inspired. We must use whatever keeps us going in a positive direction. There are going to be rough days. Nobody is "up" 100 percent of the time.

What happens in our world and in our lives causes us to pause, take a deep breath, sigh, and even cry sometimes. But as you've learned, MAPS to the Present Moment are your way through tough times and emotions. They are your internal GPS. They are your survival kit, or what I like to call your thrive-all kit to help you thrive in any situation or circumstance.

Your motivation and power sources continually bring you back to the present moment, into conscious awareness. This is where you are able to make the best choices and decisions for your greatest good.

When I was divinely guided to pen this material on Motivation And Power Sources and to bring it into physical manifestation, I agreed, not knowing what was in store for me. Though I have had questions and occasional doubts, I have continued to be guided, supported, and told that *MAPS to the Present Moment* is something that many people can benefit from at this time in human evolution.

We live in a left-brain-dominated society where *me* is more important then *we*, status is constantly striven for, judgment outweighs tolerance and forgiveness, and competition trumps cooperation and compassion. This society cares about what we do, not who we are. All of this continually erodes our self-worth.

What with the propensity for fear, doubt, and discouragement at this time in human history, it is clear that we need all the tools, resources, and support we can find and use to stay as positive, inspired, and motivated as possible. We need all the help we can get to keep bringing our conscious awareness into the present, where our power of discernment abides.

Motivation And Power Sources navigate us from confusion to clarity, discouragement to hopefulness, and illness to health, and they restore positive thinking and feeling. They bring us into the present moment, the *now* consciousness, to guide and inspire us to override our negative brain chatter and move toward our visions and goals with confidence.

My life has been greatly enhanced; I have received so many blessings. My prayer is that you will find the information here useful and be inspired to create a thrive-all kit of MAPS that will serve you well in thinking and feeling your best and experiencing true peace and happiness.

Boundless blessings!

♥   ♥   ♥

"Peace emanates from the soul, and is the sacred inner environment in which true happiness unfolds."

—Paramahansa Yogananda, *Inner Peace*

About the Author

Sande Craig's work with children began when she became an assistant in a preschool classroom; soon after, she was the head teacher. After a few years, she co-taught a combination K–2 class and designed classroom and after-school programs, which led to co-creating a special program called Holiday Happenings for preschool through to sixth-grade children.

A few years of substitute teaching turned into health education with seventh and eighth-grade youth. All of this leading her to managing research grants for the University of Southern California's Institute for Health Promotion and Disease Prevention Research.

For nearly twenty years she collaborated with others there on many interesting projects. She designed, wrote, coauthored, and implemented numerous curriculum activities and programs, researching substance-abuse prevention with middle-school and high-school students. She trained health educators, wrote training manuals, and recruited the school districts that participated in the research.

Project TNT: Towards No Tobacco, one of the programs Sande managed and coauthored, was designated by the Center for Disease Control (CDC) as one of the "Programs-That-Work." She co-wrote the training manual and trained hundreds of teachers and health educators at school districts, departments of education, and health departments throughout the United States. Both Projects TNT and TND: Towards No Drug Abuse are used in classrooms throughout the United States.

For over forty years she has taught thousands of students and hundreds of adults. Her approach has always been to enhance their confidence and inspire positive action. In all of her work, self-empowerment has been the focus and the end result.

Sande's path led her to in-depth studies in spirituality. While living in Bali, Indonesia for more than nine years, she created Earth Village Art, a nonprofit that worked with a small group of local artists to help sustain their families. She designed clothing, jewelry, handbags, yoga bags, journals, and personal and home accessories which were made by them using indigenous art and materials and sold to help them and their families.

Sande currently resides in Rancho Mirage, California, where she helps her ninety-five-year-young mother and enjoys writing, facilitating individual and group MAPS sessions, and leading meditation groups.

♥   ♥   ♥

For more information about Motivation And Power Sources, MAPS to the Present Moment or to contact Sande, please go to www.sandecraig.com

References

Quotes in order of appearance:

Touching Peace: Practicing the Art of Mindful Living (1992) by Thich Nhat Hanh. Reprinted with permission of Parallax Press, Berkley, CA. www. parallax.org.

Rumi: fair use provision of the US copyright act.

Buddha: fair use provision of the US copyright act.

Stillness Speaks (2003) by Eckhart Tolle. Reprinted with permission from New World Library, Navato, CA. www.newworldlibrary.com.

Buddha: fair use provision of the US copyright act.

Rumi: fair use provision of the US copyright act.

Where There is Light: Insight and Inspiration for Meeting Life's Challenges by Paramahansa Yogananda. Permission granted by Self-Realization Fellowship, Los Angeles, CA. PermissionsOffice@yogananda-srf.org.

Rumi: fair use provision of the US copyright act

The Essential Rumi by Coleman Barks. Permission from Coleman Barks.

Tagore: fair use provision of the US copyright act.

A New Earth: Awakening to Your Life's Purpose by Eckhart Tolle. Permission from Penguin Group, USA. jcorrick@penguinrandomhouse.com.

The quotes used have been gathered by me for years from many random sources, but I want to acknowledge again the following sources of inspiration:

- Coleman Barks—books on the life and poetry of Rumi
- Rumi—poetry found in books and on the internet
- Thich Nhat Hanh—books, interviews
- Eckhart Tolle: books, CDs, interviews
- Oprah Winfrey—Super Soul Sunday, interviews, magazine, life classes
- Paramahansa Yogananda—books, CDs, DVDs, documentary film
- brain research—information on the brain, how it works, neuroplasticity, has been gathered over the years from scientific journal articles, Dr. Daniel Amen's lectures, Dr. Joe Dispenza's *Breaking the Habit of Being Yourself*, Bill Harris's *Thresholds of the Mind*, Jill Bolte's TEDTalks, "Brave Neuro World"

Resources

So many wise ones have lit my path. Here are some resources from which I have gathered MAPS throughout my life.

Barks, Coleman: *The Essential Rumi, The Illuminated Rumi, The Soul of Rumi*

Beckwith, Michael and Ricki: Agape Sunday Services, lectures, music

Chopra, Deepak: books, interviews, lectures, CDs

Dalai Lama: books, interviews, lectures

Gordon, Gwen: Artist, gwen@artsaveslives.info

Hay, Louise: *You Can Heal Your Life*, interviews, CDs, DVDs

Hicks, Esther and Jerry: Abraham discourses, books, CDs, interviews

Jakes, T. D.: The Potter's House Sunday Services, books, films, interviews

Katy, Byron: *A Thousand Names for Joy*

Ladinsky, David: *Rendering of Hafiz, I Heard God Laughing, Poems of Hope and Joy*

Lehman, Cathy: Owner, SignWorksLaQuinta.com

Myss, Caroline: *Anatomy of the Spirit, Defy Gravity*, interviews, CDs

Nepo, Mark: *The Book of Awakening*

Roach, Gesbe Michael and Christie: *The Essential Yoga Sutra: Ancient Wisdom for Your Yoga*

Ryan, Enocha Ranjita: Your Heart's Home, a soul sanctuary, retreat, spa located in the heart of Oak Creek Canyon, Sedona, Arizona. www.yourheartshome.com

Sainz, Linda: Counselor / Consultant, www.lindasainz.com

Shadab, Lili: Event Producer, www.eliteproductionsintl.com

Self-Realization Fellowship: books, CDs, DVDs, lessons, meditations, Sunday services, Encinitas and Pacific Palisades retreat centers. www.yogananda-srf.org

Thich Nhat Hanh: *Being Peace*, interviews

Tolle, Eckhart: *The Power of Now, Stillness Speaks, A New Earth*, CDs, interviews

Vitale, Joe and Ihaleakala Hew Len, PhD: *Zero Limits, The Secret Hawaiian System for Wealth, Health, Peace and More*, CDs

Williamson, Marianne: *Everyday Grace, A Woman's Worth*, lectures

Winfrey, Oprah: Super Soul Sunday, interviews, magazine, life classes

Yogananda, Paramahansa: *God Talks to Arjuna, The Bhagavad Gita, The Second Coming of Christ, The Resurrection of the Christ Within You, Man's Eternal Quest, The Divine Romance, The Yoga of Jesus*, lessons, CDs, DVDs, documentary film.

The Internet: YouTube and Pinterest are great sites to find inspiration. Search the worldwide web for motivation and power sources. Whatever brings you to the present moment and changes your thoughts and feelings are your MAPS.

Emotional Guidance Scale

The way you feel is a clear and accurate indication of your alignment or misalignment with Source energy. Your emotions let you know if you are allowing or resisting your connection with Source. If you are vibrating at a low frequency, then you must replenish and refresh your connection by choosing a better feeling or thought. Vibrational frequencies increase as you go from the bottom of this list (#22) to the top (#1). Your MAPS will help you move from the lower frequencies to the higher ones.

1. Joy/Knowledge/Empowerment/Freedom/Love/Appreciation
2. Passion
3. Enthusiasm/Eagerness/Happiness
4. Positive Expectation/Belief
5. Optimism
6. Hopefulness
7. Contentment
8. Boredom
9. Pessimism
10. Frustration/Irritation/Impatience
11. Overwhelm
12. Disappointment
13. Doubt
14. Worry
15. Blame
16. Discouragement
17. Anger
18. Revenge
19. Hatred/Rage
20. Jealousy
21. Insecurity/Guilt/Unworthiness
22. Fear/Grief/Depression/Despair/Powerlessness

Emotional Guidance Scale from *Ask and It Is Given*, by Abraham-Hicks: fair use provision of the US copyright act.

Testimonials

I loved the part about altars and how MAPS alter our thinking and our moods. The workshop was fun and so insightful."

"What a great idea the Create to Integrate pages are. They made me realize that my motivators are everywhere."

"I'm going to use the Circle of Love a lot. So many great ideas to keep motivating us."

—comments from various MAPS workshops

MAPS engage the process of introspection and applicable self-awareness. It is something a person can do on their own without the aid of counselors, coaches, or other advocates. MAPS are self-empowering and reveal intention.

—C. A. C., Pasadena, California

Each morning I wake up to these motivational ideas. It starts my day off right! If you need a little inspiration or want to recreate your life, MAPS will never fail.

—D. D. L., Bend, Oregon

I developed a program called Discovering Your Personal Power, Passion, and Purpose that allowed students to harness their individual power, ignite their passion, and guide their purpose into manifestation. Using their intuitive intelligence, this program takes kids out of the past, moves them into the present, and gives them the tools necessary to create their future from a position of empowerment. One of the significant tools used in the program is Sande's MAPS.

—L. S., Atescadero, California

Printed in the United States
By Bookmasters